PROFESSOR ATOZ'S NASTY DICTIONARY
An A to Z Guide to the Gross and Disgusting

WALTER D. PETROVIC

© 2016

DEDICATION

This book goes out to all the people that have been my friends over the years, and who have always liked a good sense of humor, mixed with valuable information.

.

CONTENTS

ACKNOWLEDGMENTS

I am uncertain where to start since this compilation has been in the works for dozens of years.

Much of the information was gleaned from books and recently checked and updated from online sources, and much added from online sources.

I have also had many friends point out references in books, magazines and movies which gave name to bizarre ideas and behaviors, documented within these pages.

If I am to thank anyone it is to thank the world, especially the Western World, for all its sexual hang-ups which made such a colorful lexicon of definitions and euphemisms possible.

.

INTRODUCTION

Over the years I have learned, and concluded, that most people, especially white people of the Western Christian World, appear to be totally repressed when it comes to sexuality.

This conclusion has come from reading, movies, and other pop-culture mediums that use sex and sexuality as a shock value, and as a means by which to sell their product. This has become most obvious by people rarely using actual names for sexual organs, or going the totally other directions by inventing convoluted words to define some sort of sexual act, or sexual position, or some form of behavior that is meant to appear 'deviant.'

This dictionary has many actual and learned definitions but also there is a huge repertoire of gross and nasties—mostly these are the dominant definitions. This dictionary of 'the Gross and Disgusting' is more humorous than serious. Over the years, I have frequently dipped back into my files to look-up a word I could throw out in describing something that would normally not be understood by younger individuals. Today, with fewer young actually being motivated to read anything outside of short form phone texting, there is no more worry to releasing something like this XXX-Rated Dictionary because it is clear that only those people who are capable of reading, and having a sense of humor, will appreciate this volume. Those who are puritanical in their nature may find this volume "offensive" then again, that is something they will need to live with. In any case I will take the opportunity to state here that this book is direct, profane, and quite nasty.

RECOMMENEDED FOR ADULTS–ONLY!

HELP! Not a cry for salvation but a request to all readers to check over the listed definitions and if there is something that can be added, I would like to add it to the collection and follow-up with future editions.

I will be more than happy to give full name acknowledgements to any, and all, future contributors.

Contributions can be sent to the following email address: srkntwp@gmail.com

Thanks so very much and hope you enjoy this dictionary for what it is.

Walter D. Petrovic
December 2016

.

BY THE NUMBERS

3–Eyed Turtle: where you plug every orifice of a girl in the following manner: thumb in ass, fingers in pussy, and dick in mouth.

4–Front On: this position is great if you want to give your man a special treat either as part of longer foreplay or a quick warm-up before sex; massage the area between his balls and his bum, the perineum, gently as you use your mouth.

16–Horny Hound: also (also see 21); A sensual take on doggy style, this position lets him take you from behind while caressing you all over.

17–Anal Sex.

17–alt name: **Erotic Rocket**; lie next to your man, pull him close into a kiss and let him slide inside you; try sitting up together and letting him bounce you on his lap.

18-**Lust Tornado**: get your legs interlocked and pump away; extra fun—add to the fun by holding the end of a scarf and pulling back and forth to get into rhythm.

21-**The Doggy Style**: the couple are both on their knees and the man is behind the woman giving-it to her from behind, may lead to anal sex.

21–**alt description**: the woman lies on her stomach, legs are bend at the knees and driven apart, the body is turned to the side. The male partner eases to his knees between the lady's legs and puts the upper part of his body on her. The feet of the woman are fixed on the man's sides, arms are bent in elbows and she caresses her breast with them, arms of her male partner are also bent in elbows, she makes support on them and, accordingly, makes movements.

22-**Indian Style**: the man is standing, feet are wider than shoulders width. The woman with one hand embraces him behind his back, the other one she puts on his shoulder, leans back, exposing her breast for the male partner's kisses. The lady throws one leg on the man's thigh, and the second one she puts between his legs. The male partner also embraces with one hand the woman's waist with the other one he fondles her breast and neck, with a hand or mouth.

23–Hard Day's Work: a great way to greet him if he's just got in from work, hop on for the ride of your life; extra fun—use a wall or a table to support you both so you can hit all the right spots.

24–Gorge: the woman lies comfortably on her back, her head is on the pillow, her legs are bent together and lifted up and she holds her legs in this position. The man sits in front of his female partner on his knees opening slightly his legs with his face in front of the female partner's face, and his arms are on her thighs; as the woman's legs are crossed and the male partner needs not only to caress her crotch but also to penetrate into her.

25–Love   Lurer: another nifty take on the missionary position, the difference is in the way you link your legs over his or the maximum satisfaction angle; extra fun—indulge in lots of long, deep kisses.

26–Clinch Mob: just like position **27**, grab your man with your legs and pull him in. He might want to lean against a wall to keep his back straight; extra fun—have some naughty videos playing in the background.

27-Up Close and Sexy: grab your man and get on his lap for this position. Wrap your legs round his hips and let him plunge away; extra fun—lean back so he can go for your g-spot; make sure you don't lose balance though.

28-Handy Man: get his toolkit out and hop on the sofa! Just lie back and put him to work; extra fun—kick this sex position off with a bit of role play.

29-Gyrating Gymnast: woman, spread your legs as wide as possible and move around in every which direction gives you the most sensation. This can be on your back but riding your partner would allow you to feel more; extra fun—Handcuff your partner to the bed.

30-Hot Horseman: a corridor position, use the gap between the walls for leverage, and pump away.

31-XXX Marks the Spot: this is a woman's morning sex foreplay; he'll wake up pretty happy; extra fun—Make sure that when he wakes up he uses his hands to caress-up your front.

32-Frisky Fishing: kneel and lower yourself over him and wrap your legs around his waist; extra fun—do it in front of a mirror so you can see each other's face.

33–Plunge Party: you will require a table to throw your partner onto after ripping your clothes off; extra fun—strip as you go and make sure you fling your clothes around the room.

34–Here Come the Girls: you get him to talk dirty to you and touch you at the same time, perfect for a budding dominatrix.

36–G-Spot Explosion: hook your legs on his shoulders and tilt your body until he hits the G-spot; extra fun—get a vibrator up front to maximize multiple orgasm potential.

37–Throne Throbber: make sure he's comfortable before you hop on and then use his arms to support you.

39–Lover's Limbo: the man is lying down on a bed or soft surface with his legs resting on a table or ottoman. The woman gets on with her back to him and challenges his strength before he tumbles to the floor.

41–A Hand Job

41-1/2–A Blow Job: this is a blow and hand job combined.

42–Raise the Roof: both you and your partner lay on your back heads at opposite ends but still connected; Can be strenuous if you both like movement because it is very restrictive; Make sure your legs are slotted in between his; extra fun—Use a sex toy on yourself to give it an even more erotic.

47-Kneel and Conquer: both of you are on your knees or each one can be on an alternate knee

48-Love Temple: you'll need a high stool or a higher table top for this one. Grab him round the waist with your legs and pull him in. The man shouldn't move, this is all the woman's movement in pushing the guy into her using her legs.

53-Lazy Lie-In: woman is on the bottom lying flat and the man on top. This is like anal sex but the man in the vagina; extra fun—get him to massage and caress your body as he penetrates you.

57-"The Missionary Position"; classic man on top woman beneath and no kinkiness whatsoever.

58-Butterfly: the man stands straight. The feet are shoulder width apart, the woman turns back to him and he picks her up by the hips so that she is completely "open". The female partner takes her male partner's shoulder over his head on the elbow. Perhaps the position is not very comfortable, but standing in front of a mirror you will appreciate all the beauty and merits of your woman.

60–Straight Cunnilingus: one partner indulges orally on the female's vagina.

68–Bull Dogger Go Off the Deep End: the woman gets on all fours and opens her legs slightly apart. The man takes almost the same position, bends over the woman standing at his hands and legs, and kneels slightly. The male partner practically hangs over his woman, and in the process of sexual intercourse, if she turns her head a little, the couple can kiss freely each other's lips.

69–Couple Cunnilingus oral sex practiced simultaneously by two people where the appearance are like a six and nine. Can be two women or two men.

70–Mermaid: the man is standing, with feet together, slightly bent in knees. The woman stands back to him, the partner takes her stomach and lifts. The woman pulls her hands back, bends them in elbows and makes a lock under the man's arms, she also bends the legs in knees and presses them to the male partner's hips in such a manner, that her feet were under his buttocks.

71–Dog Down Submission: doing a chick from behind while you have her sprawled face-down over a desk.

80–Avalanche: the woman stands in doggy-style holding her head straight. The man hangs over her body in horizontal position, leaning on his palms from one side and the tips of his toes on the other side. This position is more suitable for men with good physical preparation. He can also lean on bed or something high, which will slightly reduce the load to surrender more to feelings.

83–Ménage à Trois; a threesome.

87–having sex with a statue or other object that resembles the number 8.

99–a reach-around tittie squeeze while doing the woman from behind, while standing.

116–Reverse Cowboy: the woman stands on four limbs with feet driven on sides, the body is inclined with head down supporting on elbows. The male partner is attached to her backside, his legs are straight and spread wide apart, one hand on the palm supports in floor, the second one is on the man's knee. For this position you will need to perform cleverly and have a penis of decent size.

140—Doggy Style: see # 21.

145–The Zombie: the man sits, his legs are bent slightly at the knees and driven apart. The woman get with her back to him and fully leans forward for her head to be between the male partner's feet and hands to be standing on her palms near his knees, and feet to be from the outside of the man's hips. He puts his hands on the back of his mistress and the couple has original oral sex.

175–Overpass: the woman is on her back, her legs are slightly bent at the knees and driven on sides and completely pressed to the body. The male partner sits on his mistress' buttocks and completely leans forward, putting his hands in front of him and making support on them. The woman takes the male partner's buttocks with her hands and moves them, setting the rhythm of sexual intercourse, the man can be watching it and even get more horny.

186–Brute: the woman lies on her back and takes the pose of bitch, she only spreads her feet on the sides and inclines them more to her head, and her arms are straight on the floor. The male partner sits on his mistress' buttocks with his arms he takes her thighs from the inside and supports her in this not very comfortable position. Notice that the man should not lean with all his weight on the legs of his woman, even though he sits down, but holds his body on bent legs.

197–Spider Monkey: the male partner stands on his toes, with his feet shoulder width. The woman stands on her head with arms bent at the elbows and lifted up, they stand at the base of the head for the support to be also on them. Legs of the female partner are bent at the knees and spread on sides, the male partner takes his mistress on her feet with his hands, helping her in such a way to be in this position. It is not recommended to be standing upside down.

203–Jackhammer: the man stands, with feet shoulder-width, knees are slightly bent. The woman sits between her male partner's feet, throws her head up, her legs are bent in knees and driven apart, one hand is on the male partner's waist, the second one is on his penis. Hands of the man are on his lady's face, with which he can perform the movements. If desired, the female partner can simultaneously fondle her crotch with her hand.

221–The Helicopter: the woman lies on her stomach, legs are straight and driven apart, arms are bent in elbows. The male partner lies on top of his lady, so that his body lies between her legs, with his hands he takes the female partner's feet, legs are slightly bent in knees and he drops them on the floor, the female partner puts her hands on the man's ankles. If you are very close, you can caress each other's legs and inflame passion even more.

237–**Hot Lunch**: the woman lies on her back while the male partner sits on his toes for the head of his chosen one to be between his knees. Then the woman inclines completely her legs forward for them to lie on the man's knees, and the feet to be behind him, with her hands she caresses her breast. The male partner puts his hands on the woman's back and holds her in this position, with his mouth he caresses her crotch.

888–Orgy.

Now you will know how to react if someone asks you: "So what is on today's menu?"

A

A spot: a very sensitive spongy area on the tip of the cervix.

ABC Party: "anything but clothes" theme party in which guests can come naked or draped in non-traditional cover-ups, such as duct tape, boxes, newspaper.

ABC Sex: in a long-term relationship when a couple only has sex on anniversaries, birthdays, and Christmas.

Ablutophilia: fetish for baths or showers that usually centers around a naked person lathering themselves up.

ABR: "**Adult breast feeding.**" the abbreviation is mainly used in the fetish world and in fetish porn.

Accident: a pregnancy that was not planned by at least one member of a couple.

Acomoclitic: a fetish for hairless genitals; gynelophilous, hirsutophilia, hyphephilia, pubephilia, trichophilia.

Acorn: 1. the head of a penis; 2. a small penis.

Acousticophilia: a fetish involving sounds; being aroused by music or a partner's moaning.

Acrophilia: a fetish for having sex in high places such as on mountains or rooftops; the mile high club.

Acrotomophilia: a fetish for amputees and their shortened limbs.

Actirasty: a fetish for sun exposure. This is often a fetish of tanorexics, fans of outdoor sex, or those who only date really tanned people; arousal from exposure to the sun's rays.

Acucullophilia: a fetish, or preference, for circumcised men.

Adolescentilism: a fetish for acting, dressing,

or being treated like an adolescent.

Adult Book/Toy Store: sex shop.

Aftermath: post coital cuddling.

Agalmatophilia: a fetish for a human-like doll, mannequin, or statue. This does not include the use of sex dolls merely as surrogates for real partners; pygmalionism.

Age Play: a type of fetish role-playing in which people pretend to be substantially older or younger than they are; includes fetishes like Adolescentilism and infantilism.

Agnosexual: a person who has yet to decide on how to categorize his sexuality.

Agonophiliac: a fetish for violence or fighting as foreplay. Men with this fetish are often fans of pornographic scenes that feature wrestling or rough sex.

Agoraphilia: a fetish for sex in public places. People with this fetish are often exhibitionists or people who get aroused by the thrill of potentially getting caught.

Agrexophilia: a fetish for having other people know about your sexual activities. This can include people with agoraphilia, those who like to have loud sex; exhibitionists, people who like to put their homemade sex tapes online, or those who simply like to brag about their conquests.

Air Inflation: one of the most common types of inflation fetish. This usually involves the fantasy of inflating a person with a bicycle pump to a comically large size. Some practitioner of this fetish enjoy pumping air into their partner's anus to create a bulging belly and a feeling of fullness, though this practice is not without risk.

Airplane Blonde: a woman who dyes her hair blonde but who still has a "black box."

Airtight: when a woman is simultaneously penetrated by penises in her mouth, vagina, and anus.

Alabama Hot Pocket: 1.the art of separating the vagina lips and taking a shit inside, and possibly having sex with it afterwards;2. "the Alabama Hot Pocket" is a special fetish maneuver that roughly involves taking a shit into a woman's vagina, typically followed up by a good ole fuckin'; a vindictive procedure where a man wearing a condom uses a liniment such as Icy Hot or Ben Gay-type heating rub as a condom lubricant, applied only to the exterior or the condom, to give a sexual partner–usually a woman–a nasty, painful surprise.

Alarm Clock: a partner who wakes you up for morning sex.

Alaskan Pipeline: the act of pooping into a condom, freezing it overnight then sticking it back into an anus.

Alberta Chili Bowl: in the middle of anal sex you pull out and vomit into the open ass hole. When done vomiting you continue with the anal sex until climax. The mess that escapes the hole afterwards is the chili bowl contents.

Algolagnia: a fetish for pain.

Allorgasmia: a fetish for fantasizing about someone other than your current partner. A common fetish among married couples.

Allotriorasty: a fetish for sex partners of another race, ethnicity, or nationality. This is common among women who are attracted to accents. This fetish is likely connected to the need to keep a community's gene pool diverse.

Alpha Male: a dominant male. A leader of a group of males who generally has first choice when it comes to selecting potential mates from a group of females. In younger males, dominance is often related to physical dominance or an aggressive personality. In older men, dominance is expressed in terms of wealth, power, and control; big-dicker, stud.

Alphmegamia: a fetish for older men. This is a common fetish among women as mate selection for females is less impacted by the age of a potential mate than by his status.

Alprostadil: a vasodilator used to treat erectile dysfunction.

Altocalciphilia: a fetish for high heels. Common among those with a foot fetish; retifism.

Alvinolagnia: a fetish for stomachs. Likely linked to the importance of wide hips when it comes to natural childbirth; partialism.

Amaurophilia: a fetish for not being seen during sex. This usually involves turning off the lights or blindfolding a partner. Some peeping toms and fans of glory holes have this fetish.

Ambisextrous: a person for whom the term "bisexual" is too constricting; agnosexual; happy shopper; trisexual.

Anaclitism: an erotic fixation on the objects one was exposed to as an infant, such as anal thermometers, bibs, bottles, pacifiers; autonepiophilia, infantilism.

Anal Beads: a class of sex toy consisting of balls of various size strung together on a string or a flexible rod. Pleasure is not as much derived from the insertion of these beads, as from their extraction. Despite how tempting it may be, anal beads should not be ripped out with the same enthusiasm with which one yanks the cord of a lawnmower; Chinese/Oriental love beads, string of pearls, Siamese strings.

Anal Bleaching: a cosmetic procedure in which chemicals or lasers are used to lighten the darker skin around the anus in order to make it match the lighter skin of the buttock.

Anal Sex: ass fuck, ass sex, brown-holing, bugger, bum fuck, butt bang, butt fuck, painal corn holing, digging a ditch, shit fuck, dipping a finger in the fudge, DNA (dick in ass), fishing for mudfish, fourth base, fudge packing, going down the dirt road, Greeking, using the servant's entrance hump the dump, lube the tube, making pound cake, packing fudge, pack the poop chute, plan B, popping it in the toaster, pumper in the dumper, pushing shit up hill, ram job, ream, rectify, rump raid, saddle up; stir fudge, third way, traveling the Hershey Highway.

Anal/Ass Sphincter: two muscles consisting of an outer and inner sphincter that keep the anus closed. These are the muscles that must be relaxed during anal sex. These are also the muscles that must be surgically repaired after extreme anal play.

Analingus: oral sex performed on the anus; ass blow, blow some ass, clean the kitchen, lick the fudge bowl, lick the jar/bowl clean, rim job, rimming, suck asshole, sugar bowl pie, toss the salad,

Analingus: oral stimulation of the anus.

Anaphrodisiac: a substance that reduces one's sexual appetite. The opposite of an aphrodisiac.

Anaphrodisiacs: drugs or other agents that dull sexual arousal or sexual desire.

Anasteemaphilia: a fetish for partners who are much shorter or taller.

Anchor Baby: the child born in the US to immigrant parents who hope the child's American status will help win them citizenship. The term can also refer to a pregnancy that anchors a couple together, or guarantees one of the parents a substantial child support payment each month.

Androgynous: characterized by both male and female attributes; Sexless.

Androidism: a fetish for humanoid robots; agalmatophilia and Pygmalionism.

Andromimetophilia: when a woman is sexually aroused by dressing, acting, or being treated like a man.

Angry Dragon: an absurd sex act in which you smack the back of your sex partner's head right after ejaculating in her mouth. This causes semen to erupt from her nostrils while she roars like a irate, fire-breathing monster.

Angry Pirate: an absurd sex act in which you ejaculate in your sex partner's eye then kick her in the shin. This causes her to hobble around on one leg with one eye covered while grunting and cursing like a sailor.

Animism: a belief that objects or animals have spirits and that humans can connect with these spirits, often in sexual ways; objectiphile, object sexual.

Anophelorastia: a fetish for ravaging a partner. People with this fetish are often fans of extremely rough porn.

Anorgasmic: a sexual dysfunction in which a person cannot reach sexual climax; never having reached orgasm; more common in females.

Antholagnia: a fetish for the scent or sight of flowers.

Aphephilia: a fetish for human touch.

Aphrodisiac: any drug or other agent that is sexually arousing or increases sexual desire.

Apistia: married and unfaithful.

Apolaustic: one who is devoted to enjoyment or pleasure; Hedonistic.

Apotemnophilia: a fetish for having your own limbs amputated.

Aquaophilia: a fetish for water that goes far beyond enjoying sex on the beach or in a hot tub.

Arabian Goggles: a "seldom-seen" maneuver when you put your testicles over her eye sockets while getting head, imagine: ass on forehead.

Archnephilia: a fetish for spiders.

Areola: the dark ring on the breast that encircles the nipple; the pigmented ring of skin surrounding the nipple's raised center.

Arm Candy: a person who is dated for her superficial beauty as opposed to her substance; Arm candy is most often a status symbol employed by older bachelors to demonstrate their prowess.

Around the World: when the woman spins 360 degrees atop her partner while maintaining penetration; ideally this is performed in one motion.

Arousal: sexual excitement.

Asiaphile: a fetish for Asians.

ASLs: **"Anus shaped lips," or "ass sucking lips."** lips that resemble the puckered skin of an asshole. Similar to DSLs.

Asphyxiophilia: a fetish for being suffocated or choked.

Ass Bandit/Pirate: a man who coerces other men, particularly heterosexual men, into having anal sex.

Ass Banger/Jabber: a gay man.

Ass Job: when a man rubs his penis between a set of ass cheeks. Like titty fucking, but with an ass and no penetration; cock dog, frottage, outercourse, the Princeton Rub, The Cardinal George.

Ass Licker, Ass Muncher: 1. one who enjoys giving analingus; 2. a kiss ass.

Ass Play: any type of sexual activity involving the ass.

Ass Quake: 1. a bouncing ass substantial enough to shake the floor. Often used to praise a thick dancer's skills; 2. vigorous sex that shakes the bed, the floor, and/or the walls.

Ass State: an estate of ass; a piece of property paid for by sex appeal; often refers to the home of a model, stripper, or porn star.

Ass Tray: an ass large enough to serve as a tray for rolling weed or snorting lines of cocaine.

Ass: 1. arse, backend, backside, backyard, behind, booty, bottom, bum, bumper, buns, butt, buttocks, caboose, can, candy apples, cheeks, culo, derriere, fanny, junk in the trunk, heinie, hindquarters, moon, keister, posterior, rear, rear end, rump, stern, seat, tail, tail end, tooshie, trunk, tush, yeasty buns; 2. an idiot who is not quite as offensive as an asshole; 3. Sex; usage: "to get some ass."

Asshole: 1. a hole, arsehole, back burner, backdoor, backdoor trumpet, balloon knot, black hole, blind eye, brown eye, bungalow, bunghole, butt hole, button, chocolate speedway/starfish, corn hole, dingus, dirt pipe/road, dugout, duster, fudge factory, fudge tunnel, Grand Canyon, Hershey highway, hole a, leather Cheerio, man pussy, nature's birth control, plan b, poop chute, pooper, port hole, pucker, round eye, rusty bullet hole, servant's entrance, shit hole/pipe, shitter, skunk hole, slot B, spunk bucket, starfish, stank tank, stink, stink hole, tailpipe, Whale Eye, windmill, windward passage, zero; 2. a person who metaphorically shits on others.

Ass-to-Ass: when two people simultaneously penetrate each other's asses, usually with a double-sided dildo.

Ass-to-Mouth, ATM: when a phallus transitions directly from anal to oral sex.

Asstronaut, Arstronaut: the first person to have anal sex with an anal virgin.

Asthenolagnia: a fetish for weakness or being humiliated.

Aunt: Madame who runs a brothel; pimp

Australian Kiss: like a French kiss but performed down-under.

Autagonistophilia: a fetish for having others spy on you, particularly while naked or engaging in sexual acts. As opposed to exhibitionists who get off on exposing themselves to unsuspecting victims, a person with this fetish creates situations in which other people may see her naked, like sun bathing nude or changing in front of an open window.

Autassassinophilia: a fetish for coming close to death, particularly during sex.

Autoandrophilia: a fetish for women who dress, behave, or look like men.

Autoerotic Asphyxiation: choking yourself while masturbating to achieve a more intense orgasm. This often involves the use of belts or ropes.

Autoerotic: masturbation.

Auto-Fellatio: when a man performs oral sex on himself. This requires a large penis, extreme flexibility, or a combination of both.

Autogynephilia: a fetish in which a man derives sexual pleasure from imagining himself as a woman. This is a common fetish for cross dressers.

Autonepiophilia: a fetish for acting, dressing, and being treated like an infant; Anaclitism, infantilism.

Avisodomy: a form of bestiality involving sex with a bird; a chicken fucker.

Avocade Taco: while you have anal sex with a girl you try to put your balls into her pussy.

Axillism: a fetish for armpits.

B

Babe: an attractive woman; also a cute pig that is clever enough to pass as attractive.

Baby Daddy/Momma: the unwed parent of a bastard.

Bachelor's Tuxedo: condom.

Backdoor Man: 1. a secret lover who sneaks in the backdoor to avoid detection; 2. a man who prefers anal sex;. 3. a gay man.

Backseat Driver: a top who tells the bottom what to do sexually while penetrating the bottom from behind.

Bacon Strips: 1. a meaty vagina, characterized by a loose labia minora that appears stretched out from excessive use; 2. shit stains left on underwear; beef curtains.

Bacterial Vaginosi: **BV**: the vaginal version of halitosis, caused by an imbalance of the growth of harmful bacteria versus protective bacteria in the vagina. The condition is characterized by a thin, milky discharge with a fishy odor that can result from having a new sex partner, having multiple sex partners, stress, douching, and using an intrauterine device (IUD). While not considered an STD, it does spread like one between women.

Ball Buster: a person who metaphorically pounds your balls with unnecessary nagging, teasing, joking, or harassing; a fetishistic act in which a man enjoys being kicked, kneed, or otherwise pounded in the balls. In its extreme form, some men get their balls busted by hammers, high heels, or paddles. Some straight men with this fetish prefer to get their balls busted by other straight men because it is more humiliating or because they think men can deliver more force; tamakeri.

Ball Gag, Gag: a mouth gag in which a ball-like object is tied into a person's mouth to prevent them from speaking or screaming. Many ball gags come with a hole in the center to facilitate breathing. A common sex toy in

BDSM play.

Ball Game: a sport in which men try to trick others into looking at their exposed scrotum, which is often manipulated to appear in a variety of shapes; common ball game moves include, the bat wing and the goat.

Ballcuzi: place your nuts in a bowl of warm water. Then have a girl put a straw into the bowl and blow bubbles under your balls. Rubber ducky is optional of course.

Balling on a Budget: a high art in which a man seduces women without the aid of a healthy bank account.

Balloon Knot: an asshole, as it resembles the clinched rubber around a balloon's knot.

Balls Deep: fully committed, as when a man penetrates an orifice as far as he can go.

Balls Out: to fully commit and exert tremendous energy to complete a task.

Ballsacking: takes some luck of the gene pool, but if you're able to do it, always great fun. While you are straddling her, take your nutsack and spread it out over her face like pizza dough.

Banana Hammock: any type of flashy underpants that accentuate a man's bulge.

Speedo; bikini briefs, Brazilian briefs, fruit cup, grape smuggler, jock strap, nut huggers, plume smugglers.

Banging the Bongos: spanking a partner's butt cheeks like a set of bongos during doggie style sex.

Bareback Rodeo: an orgy in which no one wears condoms.

Bareback: risky sex without a condom; apache.

Barely Legal: a sex partner who is just over the legal age of consent.

Barnacles: 1. pieces of toilet paper or excrement that cling to a person's asshole: chuffnuts, dingle berries, klingons; 2. an overzealous snuggler.

Barse: perineum. the space between the genitals and the asshole.

Basket Weaving: when a man rearranges his genitals in attempt to make them fit more comfortably in a snug garment.

Bastard: 1. a child that is born out of wedlock or who is abandoned by at least one parent; 2. an offensive person.

Bat Wing: when a man stretches his scrotum

out to resemble a bat's wing. A common move in the ball game.

Bathroom Denial: a type of denial play in which the Dom refuses to let the sub urinate and/or defecate. Urination denial is popular as a few sexual nerves can be activated due to the pressure of a full bladder.

Bathykolpian: deep-bosomed.

Batting for Both Sides: bisexual; switch hitter.

Batting for the Other Side/team: homosexual.

BBBJ: "bareback blow job."

BBC: "big black cock." Used in personal ads and in porn.

BBW: "big, beautiful woman." Used in personal ads as a euphemism for fat.

BDSM: "bondage, discipline, and sado-masochism." A catchall term for fetish play.

Bear Claw: a synonym for extremely large pussy lips.

Bear: a gay man who is large, hairy, and often as cuddly as a teddy bear.

Beard: a female companion who is used to conceal a man's homosexuality.

Beardo: a bearded weirdo.

Beastiality: when one takes pleasure in having sex with animals.

Beat the Rug: sex.

Bedfellow, Bedmate: one who shares a bed, though not necessarily in a sexual context.

Bee Stings: small breasts; mosquito bites.

Beef Bayonet/Hammer/Stick: penis.

Beef Curtain: the shanked out remains of the labia after being stretched like Play-Doh from an hour or so of jimmy-jam.

Beef Curtains: droopy or hanging labia minora; bacon strips.

Beer Dick: this is what most guys get after a good night of drinking. They tend to sex anything with a pussy while experiencing beer dick.

Beer Goggles: an alcohol-induced point of view, in which everyone appears more attractive. Among other things, alcohol impairs one's ability to judge the symmetry of a face, which plays an important role in attraction as a symmetrical face conveys superior genetics; queer goggles.

Bell: the head of the penis.

Belonephilia: a fetish for sharp objects such as knifes, needles, or razors.

Bezness Boys: Latino male prostitutes (Maracos) who hang around the beaches and service Western tourists; gigolo, himbo, man whore, midnight cowboy.

BFP: "bound for pleasure." A BDSM term.

Biastophilia: a sexual disorder in which arousal is derived from the thought or act of assaulting another, often in a sexual manner.

Bird Cage: a bordello or brothel; often specializing in homosexual prostitutes.

Bisecting the Triangle: sex.

Bisexual (bi): when one is attracted to guys and gals gay guy, happy shopper, playing for both sides/teams, switch hitter.

Bishop: a penis, particularly one belonging to a man who believes in the virtues of abstinence.

Bitch Slap: a slap, particularly one delivered to a hysterical man or woman; pimp slap.

Bitch Tits: a man's chest that resembles that of an ugly woman's. Often a result of obesity, steroids, a hormonal imbalance, or Klinefelter's Syndrome; man boobs, moobs.

Bitch: a woman who is promiscuous, but not with you.

Bleed: to menstruate; see menstruate.

Blessing: an allegedly accidental pregnancy that a woman decides to keep because, in addition to filling her with your devil seed, your penis also inspired her to find religion.

Bloody Vagina Belch: a queef while a woman is on her period.

Blow Job; blowie, BJ: Fellatio, when one sucks on a penis.

Blue Balls: an irritable psychological state achieved when a man is aroused for an extended period of time without reaching an orgasm. Despite what some adolescent males believe, your balls do not actually turn blue.

Blue Waffle: a blue tinted and infected vagina, made popular by asshole friends convincing their buddies to google the term.

Blumpkin: fellatio performed while a man is defecating. Often used in fetish play as a form of degradation.

Blumpy: you need to find a real tramp to do this right. It involves having her sucking you off while you are on the crapper.

Body Inflation: being sexually aroused by the fantasy of physically expanding yourself, or others. This fetish often involves wearing inflation devices under your clothes or fat suits.

Boi: often used in both lesbian and bdsm culture to denote a boyish but female-bodied person; also refers to young gay men.

Bombshell, Blonde Bombshell: before the term "sex symbol" was popularized, bombshell referred to sexual icons of American pop culture in the mid to late 1900s. Such women were often characterized as having hourglass figures, pronounced curves, large breasts, Pin-up girl.

Bondage Babe: a woman dressed in fetish gear, including latex, fishnets, collars, or PVC; . often refers to a woman who is more into fetish as a fashion than a lifestyle, or a fetish model who only participates in fetishistic acts for pay.

Bondage: fetish play in which a submissive partner is physically restrained.

Bondage: ritual restraint, as by shackles, as

practiced by many sexual masochists.

Boner: erection.

Booty Call: 1. calling a fuck buddy for sex. Often occurs when the bars close and you have not found anyone else willing to have sex with you; 2. your fuck buddy.

Bordello: a whore house.

Border Collie: what some U.S. Border Patrollers refer to a plain-looking Mexican woman they have sex with in return for letting them in across the border.

Bosom Buddy: friends who are so close that it is as though they breast-fed from the same woman; phrase commonly referring to heterosexual male friends who are often mistaken for a homosexual couple.

Bosom: boobs.

Bottom Bitch/Girl: a pimp's number one prostitute; one who lures other women into the lifestyle.

Bottom Space: the mental space of a submissive partner in fetish play.

Bottom Surgery: sexual-reassignment surgery; SRS, that involves the reconstruct of a person's genitals to more accurately reflex the genitals of the sex they identify with; different from top surgery, which is only the conversion of a transsexual's chest.

Bottom: 1. a sex partner who is submissive to a dominant partner or who is penetrated from the top; 2. ass.

Brazilian, Brazilian Bikini Wax: in general, any bikini wax in which hair is removed from the asshole; usually referring to a bikini wax in which a vertical stripe of short hair is left extending up from the vagina; landing strip, paintbrush.

Breast Expansion: a growth fetish often related to fetishes for weight gain or inflation. Enthusiasts enjoy watching breasts increase in size, often by means of animation or by saline injections.

Breast Implants: boob job, breast augmentation, breast enhancement, flotation devices, implants, stress balls.

Breast Man: a guy who's obsession with breasts goes far beyond that of the average male.

Breasts: apples, assets, babaloos, balcony, bazongas, bee stings, bongos, boobs, bosom, bouncers, bra stuffers, breasticles, bristols, bumpers, bust, butter bags, cantaloupes, chest, chesticles, chitty chitty bang bangs, cleavage, cock muffs/warmers, coconuts, cupcakes, dirty pillows, dual airbags, flesh bombs, flotation devices, fun bags, gazongas, the girls, globes, grapefruits, flapjacks, flesh bombs, hand warmers, hangers, headlights, head rests, high beams, hills, honkers, hood ornaments, hooters, hot dog buns, howitzers, humps, itty bitty titties, jolly jigglers, jugs, jumbos, kaboobers, kazongas, knobs, knockers, lactoids, the ladies, lemons, loaves, love bubbles/muffins, lungs, mammaries, mammary glands, mammies, mangoes, man pacifiers, mangos, meatballs, meat loaves/puppets, money makers, melons, milk bags/duds/jugs/makers, milkers, milkshakes, mosquito bites, mounds, muffins, niblets, nose warmers, nubbies, nubs, oranges, orbs, ottomans, pancakes, paper weights, peaches, pears, personalities, pillows, pumpkins, puppies, rack, rib bumpers, rib cushions, roundies, sandbags, sauce shelf, scones, shimmies, snuggle pups, speed bags, spheres, spuds, stacks, stuffing, sugar lumps, sun deck, sweater meat, sweet rolls, ta tas, teats, tee tees, tetons, Thelma and Louise, tidbits, tits, titties, tooters, torpedoes, Tweedledee and Tweedledeedum, twin peaks, twins, udders, umlauts, upper decks, warheads, watermelons, whoppers, window washers, wobblers, zeppelins.

Breeder: 1. Heterosexual; 2. a fertile sex

partner, particularly one you would want to have children with due to his/her superior genetics; 3. a person with many offspring.

Bridesmaid: women who are enlisted as slaves for the bride-to-be.

Bromance: the budding friendship between two heterosexual men.

Bronco: you start by going doggy style and then just when she is really enjoying it, you grab her tits as tight as possible and yell another girls name. This gives you the feeling of riding a wild bronco as she desperately tries to buck you off.

Bros before Hoes: a colloquialism expressing the idea that the interests of your guy friends should come before the needs of the woman you are currently having sex with.

Brothel: birdcage, bordello, cathouse, fish market, flesh market, fucktory, girlery, house of ill repute, ladies college, nunnery, poontang plantation, red-light house, whorehouse.

Brown Bag: a condom after anal sex.

Brown Bagger, Brown Bag Special: a person who you would only have sex with if she wore a bag over her head to hide her hideous face or to discourage her from talking; Butter face.

Brown Bagging It: sometimes you meet a girl with a body like there's no tomorrow but a face like a mangy dog; kinky outcome would be if she allows you to actually put a paper bag over her head.

Brown Necktie: you're about halfway through ass-wrecking a chick, and instead of filling up her keister with your demon seed, you pull out and proceed to tittie sex her, leaving a brown streak between the fun bags.

Brown Out: a state of drunkenness one level below a black out. One can only recall the events of a brown out after someone else mentions them.

Brownnoser: sycophant; ass licker, ass-muncher, bootlicker, kiss ass, toady, yes man.

Brunski: when a man puts his face between a woman's breasts and quickly moves his head back and forth while saying "Brunski" in a very drawn out and exaggerated manner.

Bug Chasing: actively trying to acquire the HIV virus by having sex with HIV positive partners, usually for the thrill of such a taboo encounter.

Bugger Off: fuck off.

Bugger: anal sex or bestiality. In the UK the

term is similar to sodomy in that it is a catchall for deviant sex; also referring to the act of fingering an anus.

Bull Shit: so much metaphorical shit that it may as well have come from a bull.

Bullwinkle: the sign given to a friend in hiding while doggie styling' some chick. It is performed by placing both hands over the head, with palms facing out and waving wildly. and shouting "Hey Rocky." (in the appropriate Bullwinkle voice tone.)

Bum Chum: a gay friend, or gay fuck buddy.

Bumping Uglies: sexual intercourse.

Burlesque: an artful strip tease often set to music and involving elaborate costumes, stage props, and feathers; unlike strippers, burlesque performers do not typically make a living off of performing.

Burping Fetish: a fetish for watching, hearing, and/or smelling a person burp; often related to fetishes for farting, feeding, or vore.

Bush Expedition: you invite a dozen or so friends over to eat-out your girlfriend or wife while you watch and masturbate.

Bush: a mound of pubic hair.

Butch: a lesbian who adopts the dress and mannerisms of a man. She often assumes the more masculine role in a relationship.

Butt Bandit/Pirate/Fanny Bandit: a gay man who coerces other men into having sex; ass pirate, ass bandit.

Butt Floss: a thong or G-string.

Butt Fucker: anyone who enjoys anal sex; usually refers to a gay man.

Butt Plug: usually a short, squatty sex toy inserted in an asshole to loosen up the sphincter before anal sex.

Butt Slut: a promiscuous gay man or woman who prefers anal sex.

Butter Face: a woman with an attractive body but an unappealing face. Pronounced, "but her face," as in, "That woman has a sexy body but her face looks like a donkey's"; brown bag special, brown bagger.

C

Cad: a man who aggressively pursues his self interests, particularly when it comes to sex, with little regard for others; not the man a woman wants to date, but the rogue she subconsciously wants to have sex with, particularly when she is ovulating; alpha male, rogue, rake, rascal, scoundrel, scalawag.

Cage Fetish: a fetish for being confined to a small space. This often manifests as a sub being locked in a cage, box, or a closet. The caged sub is then teased, taunted, tortured, and/or ignored by the dom.

California Cheeseburger: a sandwich in which the main ingredient is a small baby. Great picnic for the godless.

Callipygian: possessing a beautifully shaped buttocks.

Camel Toe: a vagina wedgy. Also, the impression of a woman's vagina as seen through tight pants. A common occurrence among large women who wear small clothes; when a woman's vaginal lips are visible through her clothing.

Candaulism: a fetish for showing off your partner, or images of him/her, to others.

Canine Special: liberally apply peanut butter to your dick and call over the family dog.

Cardinal George: any form of outercourse or frottage. opposition to gay marriage.

Carolina Mud flap: during vaginal sex you put your Testisticles into the woman's anus.

Carpet Cleaner: while banging a girl doggy style, tie her arms behind her back, lift up her hips, and run around the room pushing her face first across the carpet. Not recommended with large women.

Carpet Muncher: a lesbian.

Casting Couch: couch or space where women are coerced into having sex by being promised a job, particularly a role in a movie or porno; a common device in "amateur" porn where the director pretends he is testing a woman out for the job.

Castration Fetish: a body modification paraphilia for being castrated, for castrating others, or for people who are castrated; some people who have their sexual organs removed still have a fully functional sex life when they go on hormone replacement therapy.

Castration: the removal of the testicles or ovaries, often to prevent fertility and/or to reduce the effects the hormones produced by these glands have on behavior;. in humans, this often refers to cutting off the penis as well.

Cat O' Nine Tails: a multi-tailed whip, often used in fetish play.

Cat String Theory: the idea that women are only interested in men they cannot pin down or corner, in the same way a cat is only interested in playing with a string so long as it is dangling just out of the animal's reach.

Catcher: the receiving partner during anal sex; refers to the bottom in a gay couple.

Catheterophila: a fetish for having catheters inserted.

Caverject: the brand name for an injectable drug used to stimulate an erection.

Celibacy: complete sexual abstinence.

Cervix: the lower end of the uterus.

Champagne Room: a private room in a strip club that can be rented out for extended periods of time, and which often comes with a complimentary bottle of champagne; there is usually no sex in the champagne room, unless you are in a brothel or a seedy strip club.

Charity: engaging in sexual activity with someone who will get far more out of the experience than you will.

Charizarding: when you light a girls pubes on fire, put it out with your jizz then flap your arms and say 'You don't have enough **badges** to train me.'

Chastity Belt: a medieval device that forcibly

guards a woman's virginity; metal underwear locked around a woman's waist with small slits in the metal strips which allow the woman to perform various bodily function, but these are not large enough to admit a penis; see male chastity belt.

Cheese Log: the result of using Cheese Whiz as anal lube.

Chemical Castration: medication intended to reduce a man's overactive libido without actually castrating him.

Cherry: a woman's virginity; the hymen, which is often ruptured during vaginal penetration.

Chesticles: boobs.

Chick: an attractive, young woman.

Chicken Hawk: an older gay man who preys on young and feminine men.

Chicken: a young male prostitute; Gigolo.

Chick-fil-A: when a man is penetrated anally by a dildo, usually worn as a strap-on by his female lover; pegging.

Chicks Before Dicks: the mindset that a

woman's female friends take priority over the man she is dating at the time.

Chicks with Dicks: pre-op male-to-female transsexuals.

Chili Dog: when you take a hot dump on a girl's tits and then proceed to titty sex her.

Chocolate Pizza: happily discovering hemorrhoids while eating a poopy brown eye.

Choke the chicken: to jack off.

Choker: 1. a large penis; 2. a collar often worn in the BDSM scene to signify ownership in much the same way a wedding ring does in the vanilla community. These collars are often used on submissive partners during fetishistic acts.

Choreophilia: a fetish for dancing, or dry humping on the dance floor, to climax.

Chrematistophilia: a fetish for paying for sex, or for being robbed or blackmailed by a sex partner.

Chrysophilia: a fetish for gold or gold colored objects; timophilia.

Chubby Chaser: one who actively pursues

obese sex partners because he genuinely is attracted to them or because he believes they are easier to coax into having sex; hogger, whaler, whalesman.

Chuffnuts: pieces of toilet paper or excrement that cling to a person's asshole; barnacles, dingle berries, klingons.

Churning Butter: male masturbation.

Cinnamon Muff: a vagina covered in light red pubic hair; fire crotch.

Cisgender: when a person's body does not match their gender.

Cleveland Steamer: an absurd sex act in which you defecate on your partner's chest, then smear the feces by sliding your ass back and forth;. the act of leaving a turd stain on the rib cage of a woman while receiving penile pleasure from friction between the mammaries.

Clitoris, Clit: the bundle of nerve endings at the hood of the vagina that can produce an orgasm when properly stimulated; part of a woman's anatomy that grows into a micro-penis when she experiences an influx of testosterone from steroids or a hormone imbalance; button, man in the canoe, nub; the most sensitive spot on a female's lower region.

Clitty Litter: the dry white flakey substance found in the front-bottom of a lady's panties.

Cloaca: 1. an anatomical feature in some animals, that is the only opening for the intestinal, urinary, and genital tracts; an asshole, urethra, and vagina all rolled into one; in amphibians, birds, reptiles, and monotremes; 2. an outhouse; 3. a sewer.

Closet Freak: one who inhabits an alter-ego during sex that is in stark contrast to her public persona; a lady in the street but a freak in the bed.

Cluster Fuck: 1. an orgy; 2. a disorganization of people and bodies; used to describe traffic jams or a mess that must be sorted out.

Cock and Ball Torture, CBT, C & B Torture: a type of sadomasochistic play in which a dominate partner inflicts various types of pain on a submissive partner, who is typically restrained during the session; the type of torture only limited by a dominate partner's imagination; can involve stomping, flicking, pinching, burning, clothes pins, scratching, stretching, piercing, pulling, shocking, flattening, nailing.

Cock Block: 1. preventing a couple from having sex; 2. the jealous and evil person who performs such a nefarious act; 3. A neighborhood comprised mostly of gay men.

Cock Hungry: Possessing a powerful sexual appetite for sex with men, as opposed to one specific man.

Cock Ring: A ring that is slipped over an erection to the base of the penis in order to slow the loss of blood, thus maintaining an erection longer.

Cock Snot: Semen.

Cock/Crotch Jockey: A petite person who aggressively rides large cocks, as though sex was a race to reach an orgasm in record time.

Cock/Penis Sheath/Sleeve: a prosthetic attachment meant to increase the size of a man's penis; sex toys that can turn small men into cock stars but, they often dull the sensation to the point of causing the man to lose his erection.

Cock: 1. Penis; 2. a man who behaves like a

dick.

Cockaholic: a promiscuous woman or gay man slut.

Cock-a-Thon: a gang bang with multiple dicks and one or few women.

Cocksman: a sexually accomplished male who wields his cock like a professional.

Cock-Stuffing: on the fringe in gay circles, involves using thin, cylindrical items, thermometers, wire, rubber worms, etc, and inserting them into the dick hole; over many months, continue to gradually ream out the hole-at-the-head with larger items, thus ultimately allowing your "buddy" to obtain the goal of sexing your urethra.

Coerce: persuading a person to do something against their will, or without consent.

Coitus à Cheval: couple having sex on the back of a horse.

Coitus à Chevette: sex in the back of a really ugly car.

Coitus: sexual intercourse.

Cojones: testicles.

Coke Dick: an inability to achieve or maintain an erection due to an abundance of cocaine in the system; also Whiskey Dick.

Cold Lunch: 1. the sexual act of forcing yourself to throw up into another person's mouth, usually in the result of the other person eating it; 2. a man pisses and freezes his piss into the shape of dick. he then has the woman suck both his dick and the frozen piss popsicle at the same time until she eventually winds up with a mouth full of piss slush and cum; 3. to be deep throated so hard you regurgitate on your partners penis and continue sucking; 4. the act of vomiting directly onto some chick's head while she's performing fellatio."

Comarital: an extramarital affair with a partner's consent.

Commando: the act of not wearing underwear beneath your clothes.

Commercial Sex Worker, CSW: prostitute.

Community Bike: a promiscuous woman; everyone gets to ride her; slut; doorknob.

Concoction: first, ejaculate all over the floor. then have your psycho girlfriend menstruate on your semen. Stir it with your finger until you get a nice thick pink mixture. Proceed to paint yourselves up silly, just as if you were in kindergarten again.

Concupiscent: lustful or horny.

Condom Dispenser: a promiscuous woman who brings her own condoms.

Condom: a sheath made of animal membrane or latex that covers the penis during coitus and serves as a barrier to sperm following ejaculation; balloon, bachelor's tuxedo, candy wrapper, close combat sock, diving suit, eel skin, goulashes, hazmat suit, jimmy, joy bag, latex spacesuit, love glove, one-piece overcoat, pipe pull-over, plastic wrap, prophylactic, raincoat, rubber, rubber glove, scumbag, sheath, shower cap, slicker, snake skin, space suit, sparring mitt, tail sheath, tube sock, wet suit.

Congenital Hypoplasia: when the penile glands are stuck to the pubic bone, resulting in a micropenis.

Conjugal: related to marriage; often used in the phrase, "conjugal visit," referring to when a prisoner is allowed to have sex with his significant other.

Consensual: an activity that is done with the full agreement of all parties involved. Often what separates sex acts from sex crimes.

Coochi, coochy, cooter: vagina.

Copesmate: a partner with whom you cope, or struggle. A lover with whom you regularly fight.

Coprolalia: the compulsive use of obscene language.

Coprophagia: a fetish for consuming human feces.

Coprophilia: a fetish for playing with, handling, or rubbing human feces on oneself.

Coprophilia: being turned on by filth such as feces, dirty floors, etc.

Cop's Delight: the act of taking a girl in the ass, pulling out, and jizzing all over her ass transforming her rump into the allusion of an oversized, quivering glazed donut.

Corkscrew: cross your fingers, middle over index. Twist your wrist back and forth and go to work on your desired orifice.

Corn Dog: anal sex with an ear of corn after which you eat the corn.

Corn: saying that a girl is "Corn" means, she is so hot, so beautiful, so utterly drop-dead gorgeous, that you would happily eat the corn out of her crap; often used as a great pick-up line or meant to be a friendly compliment.

Cornuto: a cuckold.

Corpora cavernosa: the spongy tissue in the penis and clitoris that become engorged with blood and stiffen in response to sexual stimulation.

Cosplay: "costume play."; a type of role playing that fulfills sexual fantasies revolving around animated characters.

Cotton McKnight: inside a pussy you try to shove your nuts deep into her butt-hole.

Couch Bombing: when you fill a small ziploc sandwich bag with cooking oil, or your favorite lubrication and place it between the cushions on the couch, then have sex with the couch as if it were a woman.

Cougar: a woman who is beyond her physical prime, and who is often far more sexually aggressive in order to compete with younger women for men; older woman who often hunts for younger men, or cubs, exclusively to fulfill their sexual desires as opposed to searching for a marital partner.

Coulrophilia: a fetish for clowns or other types of street performers; Bozophilia, clown paraphilia.

Counting Games: while being spanked, flogged, or whipped, the submissive partner is required to keep count of the number of strikes; often involves some variation of the phrase, "Thank you master, may I have another."

Courtship, Courting, Court: the period in a relationship preceding marriage; the mating ritual of western culture in which a male woos a woman.

Cowgirl: a standard sex position in which the woman rides atop the man who lies flat on his back.

Coyote: this occurs when you wake up in the room of a nasty looker and you know you've got to give them the slip.

Crabs: Pubic lice.

Crack Hustler: a pimp, an actual crack dealer, or one who sells both.

Cream pie: how babies are made, which is probably why it is such a popular fetish; when not specified as an oral or anal cream pie, this refers to ejaculating inside a vagina.

Creeping: cheating.

Croodle: to cuddle, fawn, or coo, especially to ease fear or the cold.

Crop Dusting: farting while you pass a group of people; used as a tactic to get a group to leave an area or table.

Cross-Dresser: a heterosexual man who has a fetish for dressing in women's clothes; transvestite.

Cross-Eyed Fetish: a fetish for people who are cross-eyed.

Crurophilia: a leg fetish.

Crushing Fetish: a fetish for watching small insects or animals being crushed to death.

Cubs: young, attractive men who are instructed in the ways of sex by cougars.

Cuckold: 1. a man whose wife or girlfriend has sex with other men; 2. a fetish in which men enjoy watching their female partner having sex with other men, particularly men who are more physically imposing.

Cuddle: to hold or embrace. aftermath, croodle, snuggle.

Cum Bubble: a bubble of semen that sometimes emerges from the nostrils, mouth, vagina or ass after semen coats these orifices.

Cum Bunny: a promiscuous woman; slut.

Cum Fart: farting out semen after anal sex.

Cum Guzzling Sperm Burping Bitch: the once in a lifetime act when blowing a hot steamy load down the back of the girl's throat, proceed to give her a large cold bottle of your most favorite carbonated drink and make her guzzle it down. Then, shake her head vigorously back and forth to create the Cum Guzzling, Sperm Burping effect.

Cum Inflation: a version of inflation fetish in which a person fantasizes about pumping so much semen into a sex partner that her body bulges and swells with male ejaculate.

Cum Target: 1. a tattoo on a man or woman that serves no better purpose than a target to aim at while ejaculating; 2. a promiscuous woman or gay man.

Cum, Come: semen.

Cunnilingus: oral stimulation of the female genitals; also "going down on", "eating out"; oral sex performed on a vagina.

Cunt Licker: a lesbian or an effeminate man who is pussy whipped.

Cunt Rag: 1. a Tampon or period pad; 2. a person who is comparable to a used Tampon.

Cunt: 1. Vagina; 2. one who acts like a vagina.

Cupping: a type of sadomasochistic play derived from a healing practice in ancient Chinese medicine; a Dom uses a flame to remove the oxygen from a glass cup. The cup is then quickly placed on the sub's skin. The vacuum sucks the skin into the glass, creating a large, hickey-like mark.

Custard Launcher: penis.

Cutting Fetish: sexual pleasure is derived from inflicting cuts on oneself or a sex partner; amputation/amputee fetish, blade play, blood fetish, body modification fetish, goro, medical fetish, nollo, non-con, pain play, snuff, vore.

Cyber Sex: like phone sex except on the computer, often with a person who you absolutely do not know.

Cypriphobia: a paranoia of prostitutes or contracting STDS.

D

D Train: penis.

Dacryphilia: a fetish for witnessing others cry. Often a fetish of sadists who enjoy dominating submissive partners to the point of tears.

Daddy: a dominant partner who is significantly older or who provides for the submissive partner in a variety of ways.

Daisy Chain: in an orgy when participants become physically linked in a string of sex acts. Often a feature of a bisexual orgy.

Daisy Chain: partner (A) is sucking off or

eating out partner (B) who is sucking off or eating out partner (C) and so on until the final person is sucking off or eating out partner (A). Partners can be gay, lesbian or straight.

Dandy: a gay man, or a straight man who is excessively stylish and perpetually worried about his appearance.

Danglers: excessively droopy labia minora; bacon stripes, beef curtains.

Davey Crockett : a sexual maneuver in which you slip muscle relaxants into your gal's snizzpod, then slide your head in, thus wearing your partner's now-relaxed snatch-fur as a coonskin cap.

DDF: "drug and disease free."; often used on personals ads.

Deal Breaker: a negative feature of a potential sex or romantic partner that overrides all of his/her other attractive qualities, and which makes him/her undesirable.

Debauchee: one who routinely engages in vice, particularly of the sexual variety; libertine, rake, roué.

Deep Throating: when a penis is jammed down a person's throat during fellatio.

Defecate: drop a bomb, drop a load, drop the

kids off at the pool, dump, make a deposit, pinch a loaf, poop, pop a squat, take a dump, take a shit.

Degradation: a fetish for being psychologically degraded, or degrading a partner; erotic humiliation.

Demimonde: a class of women known to be more promiscuous than the general population.

Dendrophilia: a fetish for having sex with trees, plants.

Denial: refers to a few types of denial play, including orgasm denial, bathroom denial, sensory denial, food/water denial.

Dental Dam: a piece of latex or rubber stretched over a vagina or asshole during oral sex in order to prevent the transmission of STDs; one can be made by slicing a condom down the side and stretching the latex; plastic wrap is a poor substitute, but it is better than nothing.

Devil's Threesome: a threesome involving two men and one woman. This is not the type of threesome most men fantasize about, but it is what mostly takes place.

Devotee: a person with a fetish for disabled

people; the two most common fetishes devotees have are abasiophilia and acrotomophilia.

Diaper Fetish: a common prop incorporated into age play or fetishes for infantilism, scat, watersports, humiliation, dominance, helplessness.

Diaphragm: a shallow rubber cup or dome, fitted to the contour of a woman's vagina, that is coated with a spermicide and inserted prior to coitus to prevent pregnancy.

Dick Beater: an obsessive masturbator.

Dick Cheese: smegma, which often accumulates under the foreskins of uncircumcised men; so names as it looks and smells like rotten cheese.

Dick Face: one who is as unsavory and vulgar as a penis.

Dick Hole: 1. the hole at the head of the penis through which fluids flow; 2. an orifice that may be penetrated by a dick.

Dick Juice, Dick Milk: semen.

Dick Lips: as opposed to someone who has dick-shaped lips, the word refers to someone whose lips look ideal for being wrapped around a dick; DSLs.

Dick Slap: slapping another person, usually in the cheek, with a dick; often a derogatory act done during rough fellatio; can also be performed with a dildo.

Dick Sucking: fellatio.

Dick Tickler: gay man.

Dick Weed: an impotent idiot.

Dick: 1. Penis; 2. a man who behaves as if he does all his thinking with his penis.

Dickery: behaviors characteristic of a dick head.

Dickhead: 1. the head of a penis; 2. a man who thinks with his dick; Dick Wad, Dick Weasel.

Dicktator: a penis that controls every aspect of a man's life.

Dick-Tinted Glasses: a mindset that makes you see the world in terms of penises; commonly worn by feminists who see phallic symbols in everything; construction workers who can turn any tool into a dick joke; pubescent boys, and promiscuous women.

Dictator: a penis shaped like a potato that exercises total control over his dominion.

Diddle: to fondle or finger.

Diesel Dyke: a butch lesbian; Van Dyke.

Dike, Dyke: a butch lesbian.

Dildo: a penis-shaped object used in sexual activity; Any phallic object used to penetrate the body in order to achieve sexual pleasure; a sex toy made out of rubber, plastic, or glass. A dildo can be a vibrator, but not all vibrators are dildos. Generally though, dildos do not vibrate.

Dime Piece: on a scale of 1-10, a woman who rates as a perfect 10 in terms of physical beauty.

Dine at the Y: cunnilingus.

Dine In: to have sex with one's live-in partner.

Dingle Berries: particles of excrement that cling to ass hair after a fart or as a result of inefficient ass wiping; barnacles, chuffnuts, klingons.

DINK: "double income, no kids." Describes fun couples who often party and who are relatively wealthy due to their stable incomes and lack of children; also a penis.

Dinner for Two: simultaneous oral sex; 69.

Dip Shit: one who is so dumb that it seems his brain was dipped in excrement.

Diphallia: a medical condition in which a man has two penises. It occurs in approximately 1 in every 5.5 million American men.

Dippoldism: a fetish, or paraphilia, in which pleasure is derived from spanking or physically abusing another person.

Dirty Carl: taking a dump in the lil divit on the lower part of somebody's back.

Dirty Harry: a cock that is filthy and surrounded by a mane of pubic hair, and possibly featuring a prominent mole, that is still sexually appealing dues to its overt masculinity.

Dirty Knees: what a person has after performing fellatio.

Dirty Pillows: breasts.

Dirty Sanchez: a time honored event in which while laying the bone doggie style, you insert your finger into her asshole. You then pull it out and wipe it across her upper lip leaving a thin crap mustache; when a man pulls out from anal sex and wipes his dick on his partner's upper lip, giving her a thin, shit mustache; also putting a cigar between your ass cheeks and keeping it there for a few hours before you allow your friend to smoke it.

Dirty Swirly: 1. while boning a chick doggie style near a toilet, one filled with a healthy load of crap, or some hot piss, or both, stick her head in the toilet and flush; 2. a rape, while penetrating someone from behind in the bathroom as they are being sick, you dip there head in the toilet and flush.

Discipline: 1 when a dominant partner trains a submissive on fetish protocol; 2. punishment inflicted on a submissive for disobedience.

Disco Stick: a dick on the dance floor, or one belonging to a man with rhythm.

Dishabille: to be carelessly dressed, or partially undressed; the state of one's clothes right before or after sex.

Dishonorable Discharge: when a man ejaculates in a shameful manner, includes premature ejaculation or reaching climax while masturbating to embarrassing porn just as another person walks in the room.

Divorce: from the Latin word meaning "to rip out a man's genitals through his wallet."

DJ Diddles: when a person works a woman's clitoris like a turn table, constantly searching for the perfect rhythm.

DNA: "dick in ass."; anal sex.

DND: "drug and disease free," often used on dating profiles where the end game is casual sex.

Dog In A Bathtub: this is a proper name for when you attempt to insert your nuts into a girl's ass; so named because it can be just as hard as keeping a dog in the tub while giving it a bath.

Dog Training: when a submissive partner is treated like a dog; a common form of role playing in BDSM.

Dog Treat: slathering peanut butter on your genitals then having your dog lick it off.

Doggy Style: a common sex act in which the man penetrates his partner from behind.

Dolphin: an absurd sex act in which the man starts off penetrating the woman from behind, then, without any warning, he harpoons his dick into her ass, causing her to make an "eek eek" sound, not unlike a dolphin's distress call. The woman will then flop around in bed like a dolphin desperate to get back into the safety of the sea.

Dominant: the partner who enjoys control in a fetish relationship; daddy; dominatrix; master; top.

Dominatrix: a female dominant in a fetish relationship.

Donkey Punch: 1. an absurd sex act in which a man punches his partner in the back of the head as he reaches climax in order to make her muscles tighten; 2. banging a girl doggy style and then moments before you cum, you stick your dick in her ass, and then punch her in the back of the neck. The blow to the neck will stun the muscles in the female's ass, which will constrict the penis and give you a tremendous orgasmic experience when you ejaculate.

Donkey Rigged: hung like a horse.

Donkey Show: the mythic show that occurs in seedy bars of developing countries in which a woman is penetrated by a donkey.

Donut Puncher: penis.

Doorknob: 1 slut; everyone gets a turn; community bike; 2. a butt plug shaped like a doorknob.

Dopplebangers: sexual partners who look like siblings.

Doraphilia: a fetish for leather, fur, hair, or skin; hyphephilia.

Dose: an STD;. used around WWII, usually to refer to gonorrhea or chlamydia.

Dote: to express lavish affection or attention toward another.

Double Bagger: a partner who is so promiscuous that you assume she has an STD, or who would have your child if she gets pregnant, but who is still attractive enough to risk having sex with; two bagger.

Double Bagging: wearing two condoms for extra protection against contracting an STD or having an unplanned pregnancy with a promiscuous woman. Ironically, the friction between the two condoms actually makes them more likely to break.

Double Bedder: 1. having sex twice in one day with two different people; 2. a sex partner so attractive that you want to have sex with her twice in the same night, or with two mattresses beneath you to absorb the massive pounding you want to give her.

Double Blowjob: when two people perform fellatio on the same man.

Double Coyote Ugly: when you chew off the arm that is trapped under a troll's sleeping body in order to escape her layer, then you chew off your other arm to keep the troll from identifying you as the one-armed man who fulfilled all of her troll fantasies.

Double Fisting: inserting two hands into the vagina or asshole, or one in each.

Double Header: 1. having sex with two people in one day; 2. a 69 with two men; 3. a woman who starts you off with felatio, has sex with you, then finishes you off with her mouth; 4. women two people perform fellatio on the same man.

Double Shot: when a man ejaculates twice during sex.

Double Sided Dildo: a double headed dildo meant for simultaneous insertion by two people.

Douche Bag: an asshole who tries to mask his inner filthiness through superficial means: flashy clothes, too much cologne, steroid muscles.

Douche Cannon/Nozzle: a penis. The only tool a douche bag knows how to operate.

Douche Packer: a lesbian who wears a strap-on.

Douche: flushing out a vagina or ass with a solution meant to mask various odors and tastes.

Douchebaguette: a female douche bag.

Down Low, DL: 1. keeping an affair low key in order to avoid detection; 2. a homosexual who is reserved when it comes to who he opens up to about being gay.

Downtown: vagina.

Doxy: a promiscuous woman; slut.

DP: "double penetration." when a woman is simultaneously penetrated anally and vaginally; sandwich.

Dracophilia: a fetish for dragons.

Drag King: a woman who adopts a male persona, usually as part of a stage act.

Drag Queen: a man who adopts a female persona as a stage act; covers every area of the transgendered spectrum, from cross-dressers to transsexuals.

Drag: the costumes a cross-dresser wears to inhabit another gender.

Dream of Cream: a wet dream.

Drilldo: a sex machine made by attaching a dildo to the end of a drill, creating a sex toy that can spin at a dangerously fast rate.

Dry Humping: what two people do when they have yet to figure out how to have sex;

outercourse.

Dry Spell: an extended period without sex; Slump.

DSLs: "dick sucking lips."; referring to plump, moist, red lips.

DTF: "down to fuck." A woman or man who is ready for sex.

Dual Airbags: breasts.

Duct Tape Trick: wrapping a hamster in duct tape so you can safely sex it without the danger of a messy split.

Dudevorce: when two guys end their friendship, usually over a woman.

DUFF: "designated ugly fat friend." There is one in every group of female friends. She joins the group of hot girls to meet men who would otherwise be inaccessible. Her friends allow her in the group as she makes them look better by contrast and she provides someone to make fun of behind her back. When approaching a group with a DUFF, guys should always have a "janitor" available to take out the trash.

Dumb Ass/Fuck/Shit: if you do not know what these words mean, they refer to you.

Dump: 1. to break up with a romantic partner; 2. to defecate.

Dust Under the Bed: sex so good it spills onto the floor; sex so thorough and complete, you do not miss a thing.

Dutch Girl: lesbian.

Dutch Oven: entrapping an unsuspecting sleeping partner in a world of ass odor by farting under the covers and pulling them over her head, and yours as well if you're into that sort of thing.

Dutch Rudder: while a man grips his own penis, another person moves the masturbator's forearm, steering the dick ship toward climax cove.

Dutch Treat: when attempting a Dutch oven, you accidentally shit in the bed.

Dutch: when both partners pay their part on a date; asking a woman to go dutch on a date is a great way to ensure there will never be a second date.

Duva: a dude who acts like a diva.

DVDA: "double-vaginal, double-anal."; when a woman has two phalluses in her vagina and two in her anus simultaneously.

Dyscalligynia: a dislike or hatred of beautiful women.

Dysmorphophilia: a fetish for mentally or physically impaired partners; teratophilia.

Dyspareunia: difficult, challenging, or painful sex.

E

Eager Beaver: 1. a horny woman; 2. the appendage sticking off the shaft of some vibrators, providing clitoral stimulation. Some are shaped like the tail of a beaver or like rabbit ears. The name of vibrators with such a feature.

Earmuffs: when a woman's thighs are wrapped around a man's ears during cunnilingus.

Earn One's Redwings: the bloody badge of honor a man wears on his upper lip after performing cunnilingus on a menstruating woman.

Eat Out: cunnilingus; eating out—when one put's ones tongue in a vagina

Ecouteurism: a fetish for eavesdropping on others having sex.

Ecstasy: 1. a state of rapture, often used to describe the moment one reaches sexual climax; 2. the name of the recreational street drug MDMA, which induces a euphoric state.

Effie: an effeminate homosexual man.

Eiffel Tower: during a devil's threesome when the man penetrating the woman doggy style and the man receiving fellatio high-five each other; this often occurs when both guys catch each other's eyes and must high-five to erase any suspicions of homosexuality.

Ejaculate: big bang, blow your load, bust your nut, cream, cum, drop your load, fire a shot, get off, get your rocks off, number three, nut, pop a nut, shoot, shoot your wad, spill one's seed, squirt.

Ejaculatio praecox: premature ejaculation

Ejaculation: usually occurring with orgasm,

when a male reaches a sexual climax and semen is emitted from the penis.

Electra Complex: a daughter's quasi-sexual competition with her mother for her father's affection. The female version of the Oedipus complex.

Electric Chair: when a partner is bound to a chair while receiving electro-stimulation.

Electrophilia: a fetish for electricity, which usually involves electro-stimulation.

Electro-Stimulation, E-Stem, Electrosex: electric stimulation, particularly on the genitals and erogenous zones; used more to induce pleasure by stimulating nerves and muscles as opposed to the BDSM practice of inducing pain via varying degrees of electrical shocks.

Emetophilia: a fetish for vomiting or watching others vomit, particularly after gagging during fellatio; vomit fetish.

Emotional Dump: unloading all of your emotional baggage on a friend or on a social networking websites like Facebook and Twitter.

Endytophilia: a fetish for sexual partners who remain clothed.

Energizer Bunny: a person who keeps going and going during sex.

Enema: the process of filling the colon with water or some other fluid. This can be done to relieve constipation, to clean out the cavity before anal sex, or simply for the erotic enjoyment of the sensation.

Engayed: a gay couple that is engaged.

Ephebophilia: a paraphilia involving an attraction to teens or mid to late adolescents generally between the ages of 15-19.

Epispasm: the reversal of a circumcision.

Eproctolagniac: a person who becomes sexually aroused by flatulence; an eproctolagniac may be aroused by their own flatulence, or the flatulence of another person. for farts; flatulophilia.

Erection: when a penis becomes engorged with blood; bone, boner, bone-on, chubby, flagpole, hard, hard-on, morning wood, pants pusher, pitch a tent, riser, rock python, salute, semi, steely dan, stiff, stiffy, throbber, wood, woody; erection: the enlargement and stiffening of the penis as a consequence of engorgement with blood.

Erogenous: arousing sexual desire.

Erogenous Zone: parts of the body sensitive to sexual stimulation; erogenous zones; parts of the body, including but not limited to the sex organs, that are responsive to sexual stimulation.

Erotic: arousing sexual feelings or desires.

Erotographomania: a fetish for writing, particularly love poems or letters.

Erotomania: the psychological delusion in which the afflicted person believes a stranger, who is often famous or has high status, is in love with him or her.

Erotophobia: fear of expressing or experiencing sexual desires.

Erotophonophilia: a fetish for murder. A common disorder among serial killers.

Eskimo Brothers: men united by the fraternal bond of having had sex with the same woman.

Esposo, Esposa: 1. spanish for husband or

wife; 2. spanish for handcuffs.

Estrus: a state of sexual excitability and receptivity in women due to hormonal shifts caused by ovulation; horny, in heat.

Etch-A-Sketch: drawing a smile on a woman's face by twisting her nipples like the knobs of an Etch-A-Sketch.

Eunoterpsia: the idea that pursuing sexual pleasure is the meaning of life.

European Steamboat: immediately after an anal cream pie, the top burries his face in the bottom's ass while the bottom farts out the cum, misting the top's face in a aerosol of his semen and fecal matter.

E-void: ignoring someone's attempts to flirt via various electronic mediums; text, email, Facebook, Twitter.

Excrement: alley apple, baby Ruth, ca-ca, crap, dirt, doo-doo, dung, feces, poop, poo-poo, shit, scat, turd.

Exhibitionism: a fetish for being a public spectacle. This often manifests in streaking, public sex, or flashing.

Ex-hole: an ex who magically becomes an asshole after a breakup.

Expiration Dating: a relationship that has a definite terminal date.

Eye Fucking: staring at someone while imagining fucking them. This has nothing to do with actually penetrating the eye socket.

F

Face Job/Fucking: thrusting a penis into a partner during fellatio as if the mouth were a more accommodating orifice. This act often provokes an excess of saliva and involuntary tears. It is commonly featured in hardcore porn scenes and involves gagging, deep throating, and runny mascara.

Facial: when a man ejaculates on his partner's face. Synonym: money shot.

Factory Equipped: a pre-op transsexual who still has all of his/her original parts.

Fag Fucker: a man who has gay sex but who

claims he is heterosexual.

Fag Hag: a woman who hangs out with attractive gay men as a means of boosting her self-confidence; fruit fly.

Fag, Faggot, Fagot: 1. a gay man; 2. a cigarette.

Fagulus: fabulously gay.

Fangirl, Fanboy: a person who is obsessed with a celebrity or fictional character to the point that their fascination becomes a fetish.

Farticles: poo particles that explode into the air during a fart.

Fascinus, fascinum: in ancient Roman religion, the embodiment of the dick deity or a phallic charm/ amulet.

Fat Admirer/Fetish: a fetish for obesity. A broad category for several sub-fetishes: padding, inflation, stuffing, gaining, immobility, feederism, feedism, feeding fetish.

Fat Ass, Fatty: full blown fatty, heifer, hog, pig, plumper, whale.

Father Complex: most commonly refers to when a woman is attracted to older, sugar-daddy types in part because she lacked a father figure who provided for her as a child.

daddy issues.

FBE: "full blown erection."

Feederism, Feedism: feeding Fetish, Forced Feeding: a fat fetish in which pleasure is derived from feeding oneself, or another, with the intention of increasing a person's size; gaining, inflation, immobility, padding, stuffing.

Feeding the Kitty: vaginal intercourse.

Felch, Feltch: to suck or lick semen out of an orifice.

Felching: when a man sexes you up the butt without a rubber. He shoots his load, and then plants his mouth on your anus and sucks out his own warm sperm, plus whatever lubricant and feces are present. It may or may not, include kissing you to pass the sperm and fecal matter into your mouth.

Fellatio: oral sex performed on a penis; BJ, blow, blowie, blow job, blow the whistle, bob on the knob, bop, cock sucking, eat dick, gobble, go down on, fluting, head, hummer, knob job, lay some lip, lick the lollypop, mouth fuck, munch, oral sex, pipe job, play the skin flute, polish the knob, slob the knob, smoke a dick, snake charming, suck dick, suck the sugar stick, suck fuck, swallow a sword, taking the B train to J town, tonsil exam, zipper sex/dinner.

Female Copulatory Vocalizations (FCV): when female primates, including women, vocalize in specific ways during intercourse; some scientists suggest these vocalizations are a way of calling over other males.

Female Masking: a modern form of cross dressing in which men wear rubber masks, and even synthetic skin suits beneath their feminine clothes, making them look like living sex dolls.

Female Muscle Fetish: a fetish for muscular females. This often stems from a sub's desire to be dominated and emasculated by a physically superior female.

Femanal: anal sex with a woman.

Fem-bot: an attractive woman who is so emotionally cold as to provoke suspicion that she is a robot.

Feminazi: a woman who describes herself as a feminist, but who blames men for all of her problems and shortcomings.

Feminista: a woman who thinks it is fashionable to be a feminist; a woman who thinks fashion makes her a woman.

Femme: often refers to a gay man or lesbian who has an abundance of feminine characteristics.

Fetish: sexual arousal resulting from a fixation with a specific act or thing. Some fetishes are so intense that a person has trouble reaching an orgasm unless he engages in, or at least fantasizes about, his fetish.

Fetishize: to develop a sexual obsession around an object or act.

FILO: "first in, last out." a man, usually a husband, who is the only person a woman has had sex with.

FINE: "fucked up, insecure, neurotic, and emotional."; a person who places too much value on being physically attractive.

Finger, Finger Bang/Blast: penctrating an orifice with one or more fingers.

Fingering: when one puts their finger(s) into a vagina

Firecrotch: a person whose pubic hair is naturally red; redhead, ginger, day walker.

Fish Flaps: large and smelly labia minora.

Fish Taco: a vagina that smells or tastes like fish.

Fisting: inserting a fist into an orifice.

Flagellation: striking a partner via whipping, spanking, flogging, or paddling.

Flamer: a flamboyantly gay man.

Flaming Amazon: this one's for all you pyromaniacs out there. When you're screwing some chick, right when you are about to cum, you pull out and quickly grab the nearest lighter and set her pubes on fire, then...extinguish the flames with your jizz.

Flapjacks: small, flattened looking boobs. Despite the name, these are generally not appetizing.

Flash the Headlights: when a woman briefly exposes her pale breasts, nipples and all, in public, usually to get someone's attention.

Flash: briefly exposing any area of the body in public that is traditionally concealed.

Flatulence: air biscuit, air blast, backfire, back talk, blowing heat, break wind, butt burp, cheek flapper, chocolate thunder, crop dusting, cut one, cut the cheese, dutch oven, fart, fire in the hole, fog horn, gas, gale force wind, let one go, machine gun, pant ripper, pass gas, pocket thunder, poot, scud missile, silent but deadly (SBD), skunk, stainer, tail shot, talk German, trouser trumpet, wet one,

Flatulophilia: a fetish for farts; eproctolagniac.

Fleshlight: a brand-name sex toy for men that looks like a flashlight, but which contains an artificial vagina.

Flip Flop: to serve as both the dominant and submissive partner, the top and the bottom, at different times during a relationship or a single sex session. Common among the gay, lesbian, and BDSM community.

Flirt: 1. to demonstrate attraction; 2. one who demonstrates attraction, often with no intention of acting on such feelings.

Flogger: a type of whip with multiples tails.

Flood the Cave: urinating in an orifice.

Flooding The Cave: inserting the penis into a woman's pussy and then urinating inside her. Applies to butt pirates as well.

Floor Mattress: a mattress that sits on the floor with no bed-frame;. a sign of poverty.

Flossing: performing oral sex on a hairy vagina or anus.

Fluff the Muff: female masturbation.

Fluffer: the mythic person on a porn set whose job it is to maintain the male performer's erection between shots.

Fly Fisherman: a man who artfully seduces women without relying on any of the lures that traditionally attract sex partners, such as wealth, good looks, or power; pick up artist.

Fly Fishing: the leisure art of masturbation.

Flying Camel: as you are lying on your back and he is violently hammering from his knees, he very carefully moves forward and props himself, without using his arms, on his organ while it is still inserted. He then proceeds to flap his arms and lets out a long shrieking howl much like a flying camel.

Fog the Windows: sex, particularly in a parked car.

Food/Water Denial: a type of denial play in which the Dom refuses the sub food or water.

Foot Fetish: being sexually aroused by feet, to the point where you want to stick feet in your mouth and rub your genitals on them.

Foot Job: using feet to bring a man to climax. This usually involves sliding a penis between the soles of a partner's feet, or between the toes.

Foreplay: any erotic act that precedes, and often prepares a partner for, intercourse; may be performed to prolong the sexual experience, to lubricate the genitals with saliva or vaginal fluid, to stimulate an erection, to get a partner in the mood for more penetrative sex, or to get either partner as near the point of climax as possible.

Foreskin: the excess skin on the shaft of the penis that covers the head, especially when the penis is flaccid; what is removed during circumcision; prepuce.

Formicophilia: a fetish for insects crawling on you and your genitals; involves ants.

Four on the Floor: doggy style sex.

Fourgy: an orgy with four participants.

Fourth Base: anal sex.

Franken Penis: a penis that has endured some form of major, physical trauma.

Franken Pussy: a vagina that has been surgically brought back to life, especially after childbirth.

French Bread: a long, skinny, and usually white, penis.

French Embassy: a gay hangout.

French Horn: a sex act that mimics the paying of a French horn. As the couple kisses, one partner fondles the other's genitals with one hand while fisting her ass with the other, changing the pitch of the sounds that emerge from this rear blow hole.

French Kiss: a tongue kiss; Cataglottism.

Freud Stick: penis. So named as it is a physical measure of your innermost desires.

Frictation: when two men rub penises together while facing each other; cock rub, bumping dicks, frontism, the Ivy League rub, knocking cocks, Oxford style, the Princeton Rub, sword fighting, tummy sticks.

Friend of Dorothy: a gay man.

Friend Zone: a place men are exiled when they do not have the balls to express their attraction for a love interest soon enough. A relationship limbo where you serve all the platonic functions of a significant other without receiving any of the sexual benefits.

Friend's With Benefits, FWB: a friend you have sex with while attempting to avoid a romantic relationship; fuck buddy.

Frot: usually refers to any non-penetrative sex act that involves two penises rubbing together;

cock rub, bumping dicks, frictation, frontism, the Ivy League rub, knocking cocks, Oxford style, the Princeton Rub, sword fighting, tummy sticks. Frottage.

Frottage: non-penetrative sex acts that often involve rubbing. Includes ass jobs, the Cardinal George, cock dogging, foot jobs, hand jobs, Harvard Style, outercourse, The Princeton Rub, titty fucking, to achieve an orgasm by rubbing.

Frotteurism: a fetish for rubbing against an unsuspecting, and non-consenting, person; often performed on trains, buses, or in crowds.

Fruit Cup: a jockstrap.

FTM, F2M: "female-to-male." in reference to a transsexual.

Fuck Buddy: what a woman is referred to behind her back when she agrees to carry on a sexual relationship with a man who has no interest in dating her.

Fuck Butter: personal lubricant or any body fluids that are produced during sex.

Fuck Hole: any orifices that can accommodate a penis.

Fuck Off: a command intended to get someone to leave you alone.

Fuck Slam: an absurd sex act in which the top partner sudden pulls the bottom partner's legs out from under her while fucking her from behind, causing her to slam down on her stomach.

Fuck Stick, Fuck Rod, Fuck Pole: penis.

Fuck Tard: a person whose intelligence is compromised by sexual thoughts; also someone who is just plain stupid.

Fuck: 1. to have sex; 2. the most popular American curse word;. 3. an idiot. Variations: fucker, fuck bag, fuck brain, fuck face, fuck head, fuck nut, fuck tard, fuck tart, fuck up, fuck wad,

Fuckable: a person you would have sex with but not date.

Fucktarded: when you are fucked so hard that you become mentally handicapped for a short period of time.

Fucktory: brothel.

Fudge Packer: a gay man.

Fugly: abbreviation for "fucking ugly."

Full Blown Fatty, FBF: an obese person who would be considered fat by any standard of measurement.

Full House: carrying more than one STD.

Full Sail: a full blown erection.

Functional Homosexual: one who has gay sex because of an absence of heterosexual partners. Often occurs in extreme situations, such as in prison or on remote military deployments.

FUPA: "fat upper pubic area."; the hump of fat that appears on some women below their bellybutton but above their vagina.

Fur Ball: what is coughed up after performing cunnilingus on a hairy vagina.

Fur Ball: you're chomping away at some mighty trollop who has a mane between her legs the size of Lionel Richie's afro, a mammoth hair ball gets lodged into your throat.

Fur Burger/Pie: a hairy, yet still appetizing, vagina.

Furry: one who has the fetish ursusagalmatophilia, in which people wear downy costumes to either dry hump or have anonymous sex with other furries. Also includes people who likes to have sex with stuffed animals; plushies.

Furvert: one who has a fetish for pubic hair.

Futanari: the Japanese word for hermaphrodite, meaning literally, "dual forms."; in hentai anime, futanari characters are women equipped with large penises.

G

G spot: a sensitive area around; 2 inches into the vagina on the roof of it.

Gag Gift: 1. when a man unexpectedly forces his penis into his partner's throat during fellatio; 2. an unexpectedly large penis.

Gag Reflex: the involuntary reaction by throat muscles to expel anything lodged in the wind pipe. In terms of sex, this is often activated during rough fellatio.

Gag: any object used to obstruct a person's breathing or to prevent them from talking, especially during sex; a common sex toy in

BDSM play.

Gagging: most often refers to a partner choking during fellatio and deep throating.

Gaining: a fat fetish in which pleasure is derived from the idea of oneself, or another, gaining weight; related to feederism, feeding, feedism, inflation, immobility, padding.

Gallantry: respectful behavior or manners exhibited by men toward women. While this is often considered an aspect of gentlemanliness and romance, gallantry has its origins in misogynistic societies in which men were expected to provide for and protect women, who were viewed as the weaker sex.

Game Show Host: a man who has the ability to kiss women within moments of meeting them. A smooth operator.

Gangbang: an orgy in which multiple men have sex with one woman.

Ganymede: a young, boyish homosexual man; boy toy; twink.

Gape: when an anus remains dilated for a few moments after anal penetration.

Garbage Canning: masturbating into a trashcan; an efficient form of masturbation that requires little clean up.

Gastrophilia: arousal by grocery store foods.

Gay Cancer: AIDS.

Gay for Pay: a self-proclaimed heterosexual man who sleeps with men for money; .once used to describe some prostitutes and/or cock stars.

Gay: homosexual. specifically a homosexual man; Derogatory; ass bandit, ass banger, ass jabber, ass king, ass pirate, batting for the other team/side, bear, beefeater, broken-wrist, brother fucker, Bruce, buff puff, bun duster, buttercup, butt fucker, butt pirate, cake eater, chicken hawk, cock jockey, cream puff, dairy queen, dandy, dick tickler, effie, fag, faggot, fairy, father fucker, flamer, flute player, friend of Dorothy, fruit, gay ass, gay boy, gay lord, gay wad, homo, lad-lass, lisper, lavender boy, Liberace, light foot, light in the loafers, lily, limp wrist, Mary Ann, Miss Nancy, meat hound, midnight companion, Nancy, nancy boy, Nelly, pansy, panty waist, piccolo player, pillow biter, poof, poofter, powder puff, queer, queer as a three dollar bill, queen, rear admiral, rear gunner, rimadonna, receiver, screaming fairy, sissy, sister, sword swallower, twink, turd burglar, uncle fucker, woofter.

Gaydar: an ability to distinguish homosexuals from heterosexuals.

Gaynal: anal sex between men; manal.

Gender Bender: someone who plays with gender roles, and gender identity, often embodying both male and female elements.

Gender Outlaw: one who refuses any and all attempt to be labeled a specific gender.

Gender Queer: a person whose gender is intentionally ambiguous.

Gender Roles: complex clusters of ways in which males and females are expected to behave within a given culture.

Gender: one's personal, social, and legal status as male or female.

Gerbiling, Gerbil-stuffing: the absurd urban legend that some men put gerbils in their asses; most common versions of this myth involve putting a tube into one's asshole, coaxing a gerbil to crawl down that tube, then removing the tube, trapping the gerbil inside. Just as practical as a woman stuffing a hedgehog in her vagina, or hedge hogging.

Gerontophilia: a fetish for older partners, particularly partners who belong to an older generation.

Get Your Dick Wet, Get Wet: when a man has sex. Often used in reference to a man having sex for the sport of it, as opposed to other emotional reasons.

GGG: "good, giving, and game."; good in bed; giving equal time and equal pleasure, and game for anything—within reason.

GGirl: a genetic girl; used in the transgender community.

Ghetto Booty: a large butt, often acquired from eating too much fast food.

Gift Giver: a person who infects others with HIV.

Gigolo: a male prostitute who deals primarily with female clientele; chicken, Hessian, hustler, prick pusher/peddler.

GILF: "grandma I'd like to fuck." a category in porn.

Girls: the breasts.

Girl Next Door: an attractive, though seemingly innocent and virginal woman.

Girlfriend Proof: concealing anything in your apartment that may insight rage in your girlfriend; involves hiding porn and any evidence of infidelity.

Girlfriend Voice: the effeminate voice a man

adopts when talking to his girlfriend.

Girlfriend: a woman who exists in an unstable state, somewhere between fuck buddy and wife.

Girl-rilla: a muscular, beast of a woman.

Girlvert: a woman who is just as obsessed with sex as most men.

Glamazon: a tall fashionable woman or MTF transsexual.

Glass Blower: someone who likes to inflict serious hurt to someone's penis then while that person is in their greatest pain, sucks it.

Glass Bottom Boat: when one person positions himself under a glass coffee table while his partner defecates on the glass; plating, hot lunch.

Glass Slipper of our Generation: condom.

Glazed Donut: ejaculating on a woman's ass, creating what looks like a glazed pastry.

Glory Hole: a hole in the wall of a bathroom stall through which men stick their dicks to receive anonymous fellatio, often while pretending the man on the other side of the stall is a woman.

Goat: the most difficult move in the ball showing game, as it requires total commitment. A player drops his pants and bends over with his dick and balls tucked back between his legs, thus exposing a fruit basket of delectables for the player who walks in on this scene.

Gob Stoppers: fake eyelashes worn by porn stars and promiscuous women that prevent cum from getting in their eyes during facials; safety goggles.

Gobstopper: with two hands, spread your tramp's anus open, then spit a big-ass loogie down the asshole then close it back up. You can give her a smack on the ass when you're done, if you want.

Gokkun: a form of bukkake in which a person drinks one or more men's semen, usually from a container.

Gold Digger: a person who chooses romantic partners for financial gain.

Golden Shower: the act of urinating on someone; urinating on your partner; yellow shower, traveling the yellow river.

Gonorrhea: an STD caused by a bacterial infection. Its symptoms include a burning discharge from the urethra or vagina; clap, a dose, piss pins and needles, stank cock.

Gonzo: a type of porn that focuses just on the hardcore sex as opposed to the extraneous fluff in a mainstream porno such as set design, costumes, or plot. These scenes are often characterized by POV shots that make the viewer feel as though he is in the scene, and close ups on the genitals.

Goo Fetish: a fetish for gooey substances, which often takes the form of tentacles; Related to wet and messy fetishes, and sploshing' slime fetish.

Gooch: perineum.

Gorilla Mask: an absurd sex act in which a man blows his load on his partner's face, rips out a patch of her pubic hair, then tosses the hair on her sticky face, which will inevitably have the expression of an angry ape.

Gray/Grey Fox: an older man who is still sexually desirable; a successful man who dresses well, works out, and actively pursues younger women; male equivalent to a Cougar.

Great Personality: physically ugly.

Greek discipline: strap on dildo in ass.

Greek Sex, Greek: anal sex.

Greet and Meat: when you meet up for sex. A one night stand.

Grenade: the ugly friend in a group of women who will act as a cock block unless someone mans up and charms her. Such a selfless and heroic act is referred to as "jumping on the grenade."

Grind House: a seedy strip club.

Ground and Pound: modeled after the MMA maneuver, this describes any sex act in which the man drills his partner as hard and fast as he can. As in a MMA match, this usually occurs at the climax of the event.

Group Grope: a gang of men fondling each other; circle jerk.

Growler: a hairy vagina that has an angry countenance and despises visitors; bear claw.

Grrl: a militant feminist or a lesbian who confuses her sexuality and preferences for a liberated view point; feminazi, womyn.

Grundle: the perineum. The bridge of skin between your genitals and anus.

G-String Jockey: the personal assistant, typically male, and or boyfriend, of a female, adult entertainer. These men accompany their cash cows to conventions and feature dancing appearances, doing whatever their employer needs; acting as bodyguard, driver, collector of dollars, roller of posters, washer of thongs, and general bitch boy.

G-String: a thong with a thin piece of material strung between the ass cheeks.

Guilt Sex: sex that results from a feeling of obligation, such as when a woman sleeps with a man she is not attracted to after he pays to take her on vacation.

Gumball Machine: a man who ejaculates quickly and often.

Gun Fetish: a fetish for the power embodied by guns; In practice this fetish can manifest as women posing with, firing, or performing sex acts with guns. In extreme cases, it can involve a person aiming a gun at his sex partner during sex.

Gunt: the fat above a woman's pubic area, just below her last roll of fat; named as it is neither her gut nor her cunt, but a hybrid of the two; FUPA.

Guppie: a young, gay yuppie.

Guppy Face: the expectant look a partner makes while waiting for a facial.

Gurl: in the transgendered community, this

term refers to MTF cross dressers; T girl.

Guro: a fetish for blood and guts that often involves the fantasy of creating gashes in another's skin for use as a sexual orifice; also sometimes refers to attraction to people with amputation, or amputee fetishes, nullo, body modification, vore, snuff, non-con, pain play, cutting and medical play.

Gusher: a female ejaculator; squirter.

Guy with a Pie: a pre-op FTM transsexual who still has her vagina.

Guybrator: a sex toy meant to massage a man's prostate.

GWC: "guy with camera."; a derogatory term used by models to describe creepy men who use their oversized cameras as an excuse to get close to attractive women. These men often describe themselves as photographers and offer to take nude photos of models.

Gymnophilia: a fetish for nudity.

Gynecomania: a manic sexual desire for women; satyriasis.

Gynecomastia: the medical term for man boobs or moobs.

Gynemimetophilia: a fetish for female

impersonators.

Gynoplasty: plastic or reconstructive surgery of the female reproductive organs.

H

Haematomania/Hematolagnia: a fetish for blood.

Hag Fag: a gay man who prefers to be in the company of straight women.

Half & Half: an encounter with a prostitute that incorporates both oral sex and intercourse.

Ham And Cheese Sandwich: eating a woman's vagina after you ejaculate all over it.

Hamartophilia: a fetish for committing sins, as defined by your religious upbringing; pecattiphilia.

Hand Job, HJ: 1. using one's hands to bring a partner to orgasm; usually refers to stroking a penis; 2. Masturbation; DJ diddles, hand relief, an old fashion, tug job, taking the H train to J town.

Hand Relief: 1. hand job; 2. masturbation.

Hand to Gland Combat: vigorous masturbation in which a man wrestles with his dick.

Hand-job: using your hand to pleasure a male.

Handlebars: pigtails that can be gripped for support during fellatio or sex.

Hanger Model: a waif thin fashion model, whose body is desexualized in order to emphasize the clothes she is modeling as opposed to her feminine sexuality.

Happy Ending: 1. for women this refers to a romance story that ends in marriage or a monogamous relationship; 2. for men this refers to a massage that ends with a hand job.

Happy Shopper: a bisexual.

Happy Trail: pubic hair that extends from the belly button to the main mound of pubic hair; Amazon trail, Oregon trail.

Haptephilia: a fetish for being touched.

Hard Swap: when each member of an open relationship is free to have sex with others without their partner being present.

Hard-On: erection.

Hardwood Floors: shaved genitalia.

Harem: a group of women or men a powerful person keeps at his disposal to service his sexual needs on demand.

Harmatophilia: a fetish for mistakes or rule breaking, especially in terms of sex.

Harpaxophilia: a fetish for being robbed. Similar to chrematistophilia.

Harpaxophilia: arousal from being robbed or burglarized.

Harvard Style: the act of a man using another man's lubricated thighs as a masturbatory aide.

Hasbian: a woman who used to identify as a lesbian.

Hat Trick: 1. ejaculating three times during sex; 2. having sex with three different partners on the same day.

Head: oral sex.

He-Blew: a gay, Jewish man.

Hedge hogging: an absurd sex act in which a woman stuffs a hedge hog into her vagina. Just as practical as the urban myth of "gerbiling."

Hedonist: one devoted to the pursuit of pleasure; apolaustic, sensualist, sybarite.

Heeldo: a dildo that straps onto a heel.

Heifer: a large, strong woman.

Heisman: when a player in college emotionally stiff-arms a fuck buddy to keep her from wrapping him up in a relationship; to keep a sex partner at an emotional distance.

Helicopter: spinning a semi-erect dick around.

Hematolagnia: a fetish for using or drinking blood in a sexual manner.

Hentai: any illustrated work such as Japanimation, anime, or manga, that contains sexually arousing or explicit content.

Hermaphrodite: a person who was born with both male and female genitalia; people who possess both ovarian and testicular tissue.

Hershey Highway: a spurt of diarrhea that occurs during anal sex. Enduring such an episode is referred to as, "Traveling the

Hershey Highway."

Hershey Highway: when plugging your girl in the ass, you run into some hot diarrhea. Don't hurt her feelings by getting grossed out though, just pretend it's extra lube.

Hessian: gigolo; chicken, hustler, prick pusher/peddler.

Heteroflexible: a man who prefers women but who will have sex with men if the opportunity presents itself.

Heterosexual (straight): when one is attracted only to the opposite gender.

Hiber-Dating: when a person loses contact with his friends and family for several months, or years, because he is spending all of his free time with a new lover.

Hickey: appears when you suck hard on some skin causing a dark spot that looks like u got smacked in the neck with a baseball bat.

Hierophilia: a fetish for sacred or religious objects.

High Dive: the skill of pulling your Johnson all the way out of your partner's hole and in one motion jamming it home again. Best suited for use in the corn hole, but can be very dangerous.

High Dive: when a man pulls out during penetration, then rams his dick back into his partner. Generally considered a dick move.

High Maintenance: a person who requires an excessive amount of attention and emotional investment.

Hiking the Appalachian Trail: slipping away to a secret vacation with a mistress.

Himbo: a male bimbo; bimboy, mimbo.

Hinged Heels: metaphorical shoes worn by a promiscuous woman, allowing her to drop on her back at a moment's notice in order to facilitate a random sexual encounter.

Hiroshima: an absurd sex act in which a woman lies on her back and uses her legs to suspend her male sex partner in the air above her. While pretending he is a plane, the man drops his load on the woman.

Hirsutophilia: a fetish for body hair.

Ho, Hoe: a promiscuous woman or prostitute.

Hobosexual: a preference for poor or dirty sex partners. This occurs for any number of reasons: to gain access to more physically attractive partners, for the thrill of doing something wrong, or because of the perception that dirtier sex partners will be game for freakier sex acts.

Hodophilia: a fetish for travel.

Hog Hound: a person who regularly seeks out fat sex partners; whaler.

Hog Hunting, Hogging: seeking out large sexual partners; chubby chasing, pig sticking, whaling.

Hogging: 1. hunting for large women to have sex with; whaling; 2. while intoxicated, high, or just plain desperate, you go searching for the fattest bitch you can find and proceed to ride her like a Harley. Best accomplished with large groups friends.

Hole In One: the act of sticking your dick in your own ass.

Holy Week: when a woman abstains from sex for a week because she is menstruating.

Home Wrecker: a woman who seemingly goes after married men with little concern for the impact it will have on his marriage.

Homilophilia: a fetish for listening to or delivering speeches or sermons. Some believed Hitler had this fetish.

Homo: a homosexual.

Homoblivious: an inability to distinguish heterosexuals and homosexuals.

Homosexual: gay, when men are attracted to other men.

Honey in the Hips: a lady's man. A smooth operator when it comes to seduction and sex.

Honeymoon Phase: the initial phase in a relationship in which a couple is at the apex of their romantic affections. This period is characterized by overt displays of affection in public and the feeling that you would never want to be without the other person. This phase often ends when the couple gets married, has children, or when their finances become intertwined.

Hood Ornament: a clitoral hood piercing.

Hook up: to have wild sex in public while on a carnival ride.

Hooker: a street walker.

Hoover: someone who performs oral sex with the veracity with which a Hoover vacuum cleans a rug; mighty mouth.

Hooze Bag, Hoozie: a promiscuous woman.

Horizontal Mambo/Tango: sex; often refers to sex with a Latin lover or a partner who has a good sense of rhythm.

Horny: sexually aroused; bulging, dripping, estrus, frisky, fuckish, gamy, hot, hot and bothered, in heat/the mood/season, itchy pants, juicy, moist, randy, wet.

Horse and Carriage: dick and balls. So named as the dick is the driving force delivering the balls' cargo.

Hot Carl: giving a guy head while they're on the toliet, taking a dump.

Hot Dog in/down a Hallway: when either a vagina is excessively large, or a dick is excessively small, making sex comparable to tossing a hot dog down a hallway.

Hot Lunch/Karl: an absurd sex act in which one partner defecates on the other's chest; Cleveland Steamer.

Hot Lunch: the result of defecating a tube of turd directly into a girl's mouth.

Hot Pocket: when one defecates on a sleeper sofa, then folds the mattress back into the couch, leaving the turd to bake until its aroma fills the entire house.

Hot Sauce Surprise: when a phallus is covertly coated in hot sauce before penetrating an unsuspecting orifice.

Hot: sexy.

Hotdog In A Hallway: when laying the pipe, you realize your dick isn't even touching the walls of her vagina, kind of like tossing a hotdog in a hallway; frequently happens when banging the neighborhood trick or if you're slinging a small dick.

Houdini: an absurd sex act in which the magician starts out penetrating his partner from behind. He then secretly allows an accomplice to take his place without the bottom partner realizing it. The magician then positions himself in the bottom partner's field of vision and yells, "Tada!"

Hourglass Figure: a woman whose bust measurement is nearly identical to her hip measurement, with a substantially smaller waist. Ex. 36-24-36.

Howdy: an abbreviation of, "How did he get her?"; a man who dates a woman above his league.

Humiliation: a type of fetish play in which the submissive partner is made to feel ashamed or degraded. Can involve anything from penis humiliation to public humiliation; degradation.

Hummer: the well known added variation to a

blowjob in which a broad hums her favorite tune while she sucks away. The vibrations felt against your dick will most definitely produce a healthy orgasm; fellatio.

Hump 'em and Dump 'em: the policy of a serial fucker.

Hump the Dump: dirty anal sex.

Hump: sex.

Hung / Hung like a Horse: having a penis large enough to belong to a beast of burden; donkey rigged, timbered, well hung.

Hung like a Hamster: a small penis.

Hung like a Zebra: the penis of a mulatto man who is half white and black.

Husband: a man who marries a woman in order to maintain exclusive mating privileges with her; ball and chain, hubby, old man.

Hustler: 1. a male prostitute; 2. anyone who metaphorically whores themselves out. Meant as a compliment for those who do what they must to make their way in a difficult situation; gigolo, hessian, prick peddler/pusher.

HWP: "height, weight proportionate."; used in personal ads when listing your weight makes you sound fat.

Hybristophilia: a fetish for crime and criminals, especially those criminals who gain public attention. Every serial killer is flooded with love letters and marriage proposals from people with this fetish; phygephilia.

Hygrophilia: a fetish for body fluids, such as semen, tears, saliva, or sweat.

Hymen: a fold of tissue across the vaginal opening that is usually present at birth and remains at least partly intact until a woman engages in coitus; membrane that occludes the vagina.

Hyper Fetish: a fetish for having a specific body part that is absurdly large; hyper breasts, hyper muscles, hyper testicles, hyper ass, hyper penis. Of these, the most common are muscle, penis, and breast.

Hypersexual: a person with an hyperactive sex drive.

Hyphephilia: a fetish for touching skin, hair, leather, fur, or fabric; doraphilia.

Hypoxphilia: a fetish for being suffocated; asphyxiophilia.

I

Ice Cream Sandwich: when a white woman is penetrated vaginally and anally by black men on either side of her.

Icolagnia: a fetish for looking at nude photos, images, or statues.

Illegitimate Child: a child conceived out of wedlock, and often rejected by the father; accident, bachelor's son, bastard, love child, whoreson.

Immobility Fetish: a fat fetish in which a person stops moving, or is forced to remain stationary, while increasing his caloric intake in order to gain weight rapidly; related to: fat fetish, feederism, feeding, feedism, gaining, inflation, immobility, padding,

Impregnation Fetish: a fetish for the fantasy of impregnating a sex partner; related to fetishes for vaginal cream pies or pregnancy.

In Door Sports: a catchall phrase for swinging activities.

In Flagrante Delicto: in the act of sex.

In Heat: when a female's body is capable of conception. During this period hormones are released that make the female more solicitous of, and receptive to, sex; estrus.

Incest: sexual relations with a blood relative.

Incubus: a male demon that sucks the life out of a woman.

Inchworm: a small penis.

Indian Cockburn: like an Indian sunburn, but performed on a dick. Occurs when a person grips a dick with both hands and twists in opposing directions; a painful hand-job.

Indicator of Interest, IOI: a sign a person gives off, often unconsciously, to signal attraction. This encompasses a wide range of behaviors that is different for each sex and person, but which can include playing with one's hair, offering to buy a drink, asking another person's name, physical contact.

Infantilism: a fetish for dressing, acting, and being treated like an infant. This often requires practitioners to hire a dominatrix to serve as a "nanny."

Inflation Fetish: when sexual pleasure is derived from the fantasy, or reality, of physically filling a sex partner up with various substances; relating to: air inflation, cum inflation, fat fetish, feederism, feeding, feedism, gaining, immobility, padding, stuffing.

Ingénue: a naïve or sexually inexperienced girl.

Inter-coarse: sex with a painful amount of friction. Often a result of sex on the beach.

Inter-corpse: sex with a partner who just lies there, detached and unanimated.

Inter-course: sex in which penetration occurs.

Internal Astronaut: a penis, often outfitted with a latex spacesuit.

Internet Beauty: one who can make herself look attractive online but not in person.

Interracial, IR: refers to a couple or a category of porn with partners of different races. In porn, this label most often refers to black men with white women.

Intersex: a person whose bodily characteristics put them somewhere between "male" and "female".

Intimate, Intimacy: 1. Sex; 2. characterized as knowing someone in a very private and personal way.

Irish Kiss: farting in someone's mouth.

Irish Toothache: pregnant.

Irish Twins: siblings born in the same calendar year.

ISO: "in search of."; used in personals adds.

Italian Stallion: a handsome Italian man with a large penis; Casanova.

Ithyphallic: a statue or illustration that features an erection.

Ivy League Rub: the act of rubbing dicks together; cock rub, bumping dicks, frictation, frontism, frot, knocking cocks, Oxford style, the Princeton Rub, sword fighting, tummy sticks.

J

Jack Hole: an idiot who is a hybrid of a jackass and an asshole.

Jack Johnson: a hand job that is basically a fist fight between a large black dick and small white hands.

Jack Off: 1. male masturbation. 2. a worthless man; jerk off.

Jackal: an opportunistic man who has sex with anyone he can, often through devious means. He often has sex with the friends of the hot girls his alpha friends meet; a man with no moral compass when it comes to sex.

Jackass: idiot.

Jackhammer: hard pounding sex that gets the job done through blunt force as opposed to finesse.

Jacking off: masturbating.

Jack-in-the-Box: penis, particularly one that springs out of pants when a sex partner unzips him.

Jail Bait: a temptress who is under the legal agent of consent. These seductresses often say things like, "I won't tell anyone," "I'm mature/experienced for my age."

Jalapeño Finger Poppers: pleasuring someone with your fingers directly after handling jalapenos, causing various erogenous zones to experience a mild chemical burn.

Jam Out With Your Clam Out: the female equivalent of "rock out with your cock out."; the battle cry for uninhibited partying that will most likely lead to sex.

Janitor: a wingman who has sex with the ugly friend in a group of women so that his friend(s) can get the ugly girl's attractive friend(s) alone;. named because a janitor takes out the trash. Although the term sounds derogatory, the janitor serves a vital function, much like real janitors.

Jawbreaker: a large penis.

Jelly Belly: ejaculating on a partner's stomach.

Jerk Off: 1. male masturbation; 2. a worthless man; jack off.

Jersey Turnpike: an absurd sex act in which you stick a finger in your partner's ass, then stick that finger in your partner's mouth. If you later forget to wash your hands and put that finger anywhere near your face, the mistake is referred to as "Taking the Newark Exit."

Jilling off, missterbation, buffin' the muffin, petting the bunny: female masturbation

Jizz Whistle: penis.

Jizz: 1. Semen; 2. the act of ejaculating.

Jizzing: cumming.

JO: "jerk off."; used in personal ads, indicates a desire to engage in simultaneous masturbation.

John: a prostitute's customer.

Johnny Bench Called: an abbreviation of the statement, "Johnny Bench Called and he want his catcher's mitt back." A way of saying a woman has an old, worn out vagina, comparable to the catcher's mitt of one of the greatest baseball catchers of all time.

Joined at the Dick: two heterosexual men who spend as much time together as a romantic couple.

Joined at the Groin: sex.

Joy Juice: natural female lubrication.

Jump Start: to wake a partner or to get them in the mood for sex with foreplay.

Jumping on the Grenade: when a wingman sacrifices his penis by having sex with an ugly woman so that his friend(s) may have sex with the grenade's attractive friend(s); disarming the Bomb.

Jungle Fever: a sexual appetite for a member of another race; often refers to a white person's preference for an African type.

Junk in the Trunk: large ass.

Just the Tip: gateway foreplay that leads to intercourse. This occurs when a partner is hesitant about being penetrated, especially without a condom. The eager male promises just to put the tip of his penis in, just for a moment, just to see how it feels. Full penetration soon follows.

K

Kennebunkport Surprise: The tact of secretly filling your cheeks with chunky-style New England clam chowder, and screaming in disgust as you hurl it between your partners legs while eating her out.

Kentucky Fried Dicking: during a particularly sloppy blow job, the man dips his saliva-coated penis in any number of dry food products, like bread crumbs or flour, then sticks the treat back in his partner's mouth.

Kentucky Klondike Bar: the act of 'freezing' a bowel movement and sexually penetrating another with the frozen bowel movement.

Keptie: a mistress; a kept woman.

Key Party: a swinger party where each couple places a house key in a bowl then picks one out randomly at the end of the night to determine who will go home with who.

Kicking the Tires: premarital sex; from the practice of kicking the tires of a used car before purchasing it.

Kick-Sexing: the act of receiving sexual pleasure from repeatedly getting kicked in the ass.

Kigurumi: a fetish involving anime masks. This most often manifests as men dressing up as female anime characters.

Kinesophilia: a fetish for exercise: See coregasm and sexercise.

Kink: a preference for the unconventional, especially when it comes to sex; from a kink in a rope, possibly related to the popular kink of bondage or whipping.

Kinky: open to a variety of sex acts that many people may consider devious.

Kiss Ass: a sycophant, does anything for someone.

Kleptophilia: a fetish for stealing.

Klingons: pieces of toilet paper or excrement that cling to a person's asshole; chuffnuts, barnacles, dingle berries.

Klismaphilia: a fetish for enemas.

Knee Trembler: vigorous sex while standing that leaves your legs shaking.

Knismolagnia, Knismo: a fetish for ticking others or being tickled.

Knissophilia: a fetish for incense.

Kokigami: the wrapping of a penis in a paper costume.

Kooch, koochi, koochy: vagina; cooch, coochie, coochy.

Koro: a psychological disorder in which a person believes his or her genitals are shrinking and retracting into the body.

Kumquat: a sexy woman, usually of Asian descent; the Asian fruit of the same name.

KY: personal lubrication; from one of the first and most popular brands of lube.

L

Labia Majora: large folds of skin that run downward from the mons along the sides of the vulva; the thicker, outer lips of the vagina; "the lips".

Labia Minora: the thin, inner folds of skin within the outer vaginal lips; nymphae.

Lace Curtain: foreskin.

Lacka Nookie: the Hawaiian disease of not getting any.

Lactation Fetish: a fetish for lactating breasts. Fans of this fetish often want to nurse, be milked, or milk their partner; relating to infantilism, pregnancy fetish, hyper breasts, breast expansion, or wet and messy fetishes.

Lactoids: breasts.

Lactophilia: a fetish for breast milk.

Lady Boner: when a woman is sexually aroused.

Landing Strip: a thin line of pubic hair extending up from a woman's vagina.

Landshark: the woman braces herself facing a wall, naked, hands against the wall, legs spread, bent over so that her ass is lusciously jutting out, the guy also naked as well as stiff cocked, walks to the opposite end of the room, places his palms together and raises them above his head, imitating the dorsal fin of a shark, and begins chanting the theme to Jaws. When given some predetermined signal, the guy sprints toward the girl at full speed with his pelvis-out, fin protruding, and rams her dead square in the ass.

Leather Cheerio: asshole.

Lecher: a man who is obsessed with having sex with women; alley cat, bed presser, bum fiddler, Casanova, chimney sweep, cocksman, cocksmith, Don Juan, fleece hunter, flesh monger, fox hunter, fuckster, lech, libertine, lothario, sportsman, swordsman, tomcat, whore hound, womanizer, woodman.

Lecherous: obsessive or offensive sexual desires; carnal, concupiscent, corrupt, fast, hot and heavy, incontinent, lascivious, lewd, libertine, libidinous, licentious, low-down, lubricous, lustful, prurient, raunchy, salacious, satyric, sensual, unchaste, wanton.

Lemon Tart: a promiscuous blonde.

Lesbian: a woman who is sexually attracted to other women; Slurs: bull, bull dyke, butch, beaver eater, carpet muncher, cunt licker, cunt lover, dike, dyke, diesel dyke, gal boy, les, lesbo, lezzie, muff diver, rug eater.

Lesbophilia: a fetish among men who are aroused by girl-on-girl sex; can refer to men who like to image themselves as lesbians.

Lexis: the 69 sex position; as in the Roman numerals for 69, LXIX.

Liberace: a flamboyant gay man given to dramatics.

Libertine: one who pursues carnal pleasures with little concern for the social or moral constraints of his time; a freethinker. Examples: Marquis de Sade; debauchee, rake, roué

Lick the Bowl/Jar (Clean): analingus.

Light in the Loafers: a gay man.

Lilith Position: intercourse with the woman on top, man on bottom.

Limp Biscuit: a game of circle jerk in which the players race to ejaculate on a cracker in the center of the circle. The last man to finish must eat the soggy biscuit.

Limp Wristed: a gay man.

Lingerie: sexually arousing underwear that accentuates the good and hides the bad parts of a woman's physique, such as lifting her breasts and compressing her stomach.

Lip Crispies: a lesion of oral herpes.

Lipstick Lesbian: a woman who dates and marries men but who will kiss or have sex with other attractive women for attention, to get off, or for money; most all female porn stars are lipstick lesbians. These women represent the heterosexual fantasy of what lesbians are.

Liptease: the act of applying lipstick or eating dick-shaped food in a sexually provocative way.

Literotica: literary erotica; a genre of creative writing.

Load: semen.

Lobster: a man who is notorious for pinching women's asses.

Lock Crotches: sex; joined at the Groin.

Lolicon: a trend in hentai porn that revolves around young Japanese girls. The focus is more on the innocence of the character, or her lack of sexual development, as opposed to her actual age. Loli characters are often depicted as having flat chests, wide hips, and subtle curves.

Lollipop Stop: a truck strop frequented by prostitutes, who are known as lot lizards.

London Bridge: a group sex act in which two men penetrate women from behind while the women kiss each other.

Look Both Ways: to ogle a woman inconspicuously.

Looner, Looning: a person with a fetish for balloon popping.

Loose Change: a fuck buddy you call when no other options are available; used when you are down on your luck, like loose change or a pay phone.

Lordosis: a mating posture displayed by many female mammals, such as rats or cats; usually the receptive female arches her back and displays her ass, inviting sex.

Lorena Bobbit: during anal sex, the receiving partner squeezes her ass cheeks together in attempt to snap off the man's penis.

Lot Lizard: 1. a prostitute who solicits customers at truck stops; 2. a woman who flirts her way from group to group at a tailgate or other outdoor gathering in search of free food, drugs, or alcohol.

Love Glove: condom.

Love Muscle: penis.

Love Wand: vibrator.

LTR: "Long term relationship."; used in personal ads.

Lube the Tube: anal sex.

LUG: "Lesbian until graduation." a woman who sleeps with other women in college, but then dates men; a hasbian.

Lunch Break, Lunch Meet/Meat, Luncher: a quickie during your lunch break. Often occurs in a car with a co-worker; nooner, quick lube.

Luppie: a lesbian yuppie.

Lush: someone who often gets drunk and overly flirtatious.

Lust: sexual desire; luxuria.

Luxuria: lust as a sin; unrestrained desire.

M

Mack Daddy: 1. a lady's man; 2. a pimp.

Mack: 1. to successfully flirt with one or more women; 2. a pimp; 3. the act of pimping, in the metaphorical or literal sense.

Macro Fetish: a fetish for giant, though not necessarily obese, sex partners; often reserved for the realm of anime or fantasy; vore, crushing, or growth fetish.

Macrogenitalism: a fetish for large genitals; phallophilia.

Macrophilia: a fetish for giants; often involves the fantasy of being at the complete mercy of a much larger sex partner.

Madam's Apple: an Adam's apple that gives away a MTF transsexual.

Madame: a woman who runs a brothel; aunt, pimp.

Magic Wand/Stick: 1. penis; 2. vibrator.

Mail Order Bride: generally a woman from an impoverished country who agrees to marry a foreigner with the express intention of economic betterment.

Make Love/Babies/It/Whoopee: some of the most inoffensive euphemisms for sex.

Make Out: to tongue kiss for an extended period.

Man Hole Cover: a Tampon or period pad.

Manal: anal sex performed on a man.

Mandy: man candy; a man who is kept around for sexual or dating purposes, primarily because of his physical beauty or sexual skills as opposed to his success, personality, or wealth.

Man-gerie: lingerie made for and worn by men.

Mangina: formed when a man tucks his dick and balls behind his legs.

Manible: an animalistic man; one of the highest compliments a man can bestow on another man; refers to athletes who are so manly, they behave like wild animals.

Manscape: when a man grooms and trims his body hair; a male body that has been expertly landscaped.

Mantsy: horny, or antsy, for men; cock craving.

Manwich: a devil's threesome with two men and one woman; related to an ice cream sandwich.

Marital Aid: 1. a vibrator; 2. an inoffensive term for any sex toy.

Maschalagnia: a fetish for smelling armpits.

Masochism: a fetish for being subservient to a dominant partner who delivers physical or emotional abuse.

Massachusetts Slurpee: when during intercourse, right before the girl climaxes, you whip out a straw and put it into her vagina. Once the straw is tightly shoved in, you start masturbating until you can perform a 'money shot' into the straw, which funnels down into her vagina.

Mastectomy: the surgical removal of one or both breasts, usually as a way of fighting breast cancer.

Master: the dominant partner in fetish play. Often used as a title the submissive partner must use in reference to the dominant partner. Ex. Master Honey Badger.

Masturbation: bringing oneself to orgasm.
-Unisex Masturbation: celebrate the celibate, couch hockey, devil's handshake, diddle, feel your way around, five knuckle shuffle, fly fishing, get to know yourself, give yourself a low five, hand jive, hand job, hand relief, hand to gland combat, hands-on training, hand work, hitchhike to heaven, honk your horn, manual override/labor, one-handed clap, pack your palm, practice safe sex, rub one out, rub Buddha's tummy, scratch an itch, secret handshake, self abuse, sex with someone you love, solo sex, staff meeting, take matters into your own hands, take part in population control, tend to your own affairs, test your batteries, work out a cramp/ things out with yourself, wrist aerobics

-Male Masturbation:

A: adjust the antenna, aid and abet a known felon, answer the bone, apply the hand brake, assault on a friendly weapon, audition your hand puppet.

B: backstroke roulette, badger the witness, bait the hook, bash the bishop, baste the ham, batting practice, battle the purple-headed yogurt slinger, beat off, beat the bishop/bologna/meat/your date, be your own best friend, blow your horn/load, bludgeon the beefsteak, bop bonzo, buff the banister/bananas, build upper body strength, burp the baby/worm, butter the corn.

C: caulk the cracks in the bathroom tile, change the oil, charm the cobra/snake, cheese off, check for testicular cancer/ticks, choke the chicken/turkey/Kojak, choke the sheriff and wait for the posse to come, churn butter, clean out your account, clean the pipes/rifle, clear the snorkel, combing the hair on your blind pig, commune with nature, consult with your silent partner, corral your tadpole, couch hockey for one, crank the shank/yank/love pump, crown the king, cuddle the kielbasa.

D: dance with the one-eyed sailor, Day-out with the Cyclops; date Pam Handerson/Miss; Michigan/Fisty: Plamer/Handrea, and Palmela/Madame Palm and her five daughters/Rosie Palm and her five sisters/Mother Thumb and her four daughters, deploy the troops, discover your potential, dishonorable discharge, disseminate, doddle the noodle, do handiwork, do it your way, do some janitorial work, do your homework, drain the monster/vein, dry hump the ottoman.

E: engage in safe sex.

F: fiddle/finger the flesh flute, five against one, five knuckle shuffle, flog the dog/the hog/your dong/the bishop/the dolphin, flute solo, free willy, frost the pastries.

G: get in touch with your manhood, give it a tug, go blind, Go Hans Solo on Darth Vader's head, goose the gherkin, grease the pipe/hog.
H: hard labor, hold the sausage hostage, hug your hog.

I: iron out some wrinkles; irritate Hank, irrigate the field.

J: jack hammer, jackin' the beanstalk, jack off, jerk off, jerking the gherkin, jiggle the jewels.

L: liquidate the inventory; launch the rocket.

M: make the bald man cry/puke, make bread rise/a milkshake/chowder with sailor Ned /stomach pancakes /nut, manipulate mandingo, butter /yogurt /soup, manhandle/mangle/manage the midget, , massage your muscle, measure for condoms, milk the cow /lizard /moose/monkey, much goo about nothing.

N: null the void.

O: oil the glove, one-man show/rodeo/tug of war/band, one gun salute, one man.

P: pack your palm, paddle the pickle/prince, paint the pickle/ceiling, Pam Anderson Polka, peel the banana, pet the lizard, play the piccolo/organ/skin flute/with dick/a little five-on-one/a one stringed guitar/in a one-man show/peek-a-boo/it safe, please the pisser, polish the rocket/sword, pocket pinball, pocket pool/pinball, polish the sword/family jewels/the helmet/the rocket, pound off/the flounder/the pud/the fence post, prime the pump, pull rank/the pole/taffy/your own leg/your own weight, pump the python/the stump, punch the munchkin, putting Mr. Kleenex's kids through college.

Q: queen's Salute, quitting the army, quench the parch.

R: relish your hot dog, roll your own/the Bologna, roman helmet rumba, rope the pony/pope, round up the tadpoles.

S: salute the general, sample the secret sauce, season the meat, self-induced penile regurgitation, shake hands with the midget/your wife's best friend, shake the sausage/snake, shine the pole/helmet/sword, shoot yourself in the foot/airplanes/for the moon/putty at the moon, chuck your corn, slam the spam/salami/ham/salmon, slap box the one-eyed champ/the cyclops, sling jelly, smack the salami, solo flight, spank the frank/monkey, spread the Mayo, squeeze cream from the Twinkie/the toothpaste/your cheese-dog, soldier's joy, start a crotch fire, stir the batter/yogurt, stroke it/off, stroke the goat/dog/poke, strum the one-stringed guitar.

T: take a shake break/a few practice swings/a load off, tame the snake/hog/shrew, taunt the cyclops, tease the weasel, tenderize the tube steak, thread the needle, thump the pump, tickle elmo, tickle the pickle, toss off, toss the boss, tug the tapioca tube, tug of war with the baby arm, tune the antenna, tussle with the muscle.

U: unload the single-shot.

V: varnish the flagpole/banister, visit Rosie Palm and her five daughters.

W: wail away, walk the dog/willy the wonder worm, wallow in self-pity, wank, wank the snake, wash the meat, wax the weasel, whack off, whip the pony, whip your dripper/the stiff/up some cream, whitewash the fence, whittle the stick, whizzing jizzim, wiggle the worm, wind the jack-in-the-box, work willy/up a nice lather, wrestle the weasel, wring out the rope.

X,Y,Z: yank, yank the doodle/crank/plank/yam.

—**Female Masturbation**: beat the beaver, clap the clit, finger fuck, fluff the muff, get in touch with your feminine side, grease the gash, paddle the pink canoe, pet the poodle, rub one out, slam the clam, tickle the taco, two-finger tango, vagina monologue, vibing out, waxing the turtle shell, Masturbation: sexual self-stimulation.

Master-Slave Relationship: an ongoing, fetishistic relationship between a dominant and submissive partner.

Mastrophobia: a fear of breasts.

Mating Ritual: general behavior performed by most members of a species in regards to mating. In non-human animals, this behavior is easily recognizable, such as the male Bowerbird decorating his nest with blue objects to entice a female or Albatrosses performing a dance with their partner.

Mating Strategy: various tactics used to secure sex partners. These are usually employed by less desirable members of a species to compensate for their shortcomings, or to secure a mate who has a higher social value. Human Beta males do such things as develop senses of humor, secure high paying jobs, or date women who have children from another man. Beta females may employ such strategies as being more sexually aggressive than their more attractive counterparts, playing hard to get, or getting breast implants.

Mature: 1. what a woman mistakenly believes she and her sex partner are when she dates a man who is significantly older; 2. used in porn and personal ads as a euphemism for old.

MBA: "Married but available." often used on alternative dating websites.

Meal On Wheels: oral sex in a moving car; road head.

Meat Hound: one who has an insatiable appetite for man-meat; Cock Hound.

Meat Market: any place where people go to show off their bodies and to shop for sex partners.

Mechanophila: a fetish for machines like cars, bikes, or gadgets.

Medical Play: erotic, fetishistic behavior involving medical equipment. Often involves role playing as the dominant doctor/nurse and the submissive patient. This encompasses a wide range of acts, such as fake gynecological exams to administering enemas.

Medusa: an ugly woman who has the magical ability to turn a man's dick to stone.

Megalophilia: a fetish for large objects.

Melolagnia: a fetish for music. When a person becomes sexually aroused by music.

Melon Dive: leaping face first into boobs. Similar to motor boating except it is often done without consent. A common move at strip clubs.

Melon Smuggler: a woman who wears outfits that mask the full splendor of her large breasts.

Ménage à Trois: threesome.

Menglish: coded language used by men to talk about sex and females in the presence of women.

Menstruation: aunt flo, aunt rosie, all's not quiet on the waterfront, bleed, blood week, cracking an egg, curse of eve, drip, flying the red flag, holy week, monthlies, on the bun, on the rag, period, ragtime, red flag, riding the cotton pony, stop sign, tail flowers, the curse, the plague, the visitor, woman's home companion,

Menthol: performing oral sex while chewing strong breath mints or gum in order to create a tingling sensation.

Merinthophilia: a fetish for bondage; vincilagnia.

Merkin: 1. a pubic wig; 2. someone who tries to conceal her lasciviousness.

Metrophilia: a fetish for poetry.

Micro Fetish: a fetish for being small, or for engaging in sex play with small partners. This is often related to macro fetishes, as the person often enjoys imagining that he is small in comparison to his giant object of worship. Practitioners of this fetish often like to be smothered or crushed by various body parts of a larger partner; related to vore and crushing.

Micropenis, Microphallus: a penis that is 2.5 standard deviations below the average penis length for the age of the individual. A micropenis for an adult is around 7 cm or less.

Midnight Cowboy: a gigolo.

Mighty Mouth: a master of the art of oral sex; hoover.

MILF: "mom I'd Like to Fuck."; a popular category of porn.

Milk Man's Kids: offspring who do not resemble their alleged biological father.

Milking: the act of getting a man to ejaculate through hand stimulation; can refer to a hand job that mimics the milking of a cow, or the milking of the prostate through anal stimulation.

Mint: a perfect specimen of sexiness.

Missionary Position: the most basic sex position. The woman lies on her back while the man penetrates her from above; mish.

Missouri Backwash: after giving a guy a blow job and having him blow a loud into your mouth, you then spit the jizz back at his face.

Mister Reliable: a vibrator.

Mixophilia: a fetish for watching a partner or yourself engage in sexual activity. This fetish often involves mirrors or sex tapes.

Mofo: "mother fucker."

Mojo: masculine charm and charisma. The power that gives men the ability to seduce.

Monday Morning Rebound Syndrome: the

regret that kicks in when you resume your professional life after a weekend of experimenting with various sexual taboos.

Money Shot: when a man ejaculates, especially on his partner's face; this is the one crucial shot in a porno; facial.

Monkey Wrench: when a dick is pulled back between a man's legs and sucked off.

Monkey Wrench: when some sadistic lady takes your dick back between your legs and sucks you off.

Monroe Transfer: when you and your partner connect each other's assholes with a tube. One defecates through the tube, thus transferring the turds to the rectum of the other.

Mons Veneris: a mound of fatty tissue that covers the joint of the pubic bones in front of the body, below the abdomen and above the clitoris.

Monster Fetish: a fetish for a wide range of monstrous creatures. Practitioners of this fetish often enjoy the fantasy of being dominated by a monster.

Moobs: man boobs.

Moose Knuckle: the lumpy bulge that appears when a man wears too tight of pants. Brother of the camel toe.

Moped: an embarrassing sex partner. So named because, like a moped, such a partner is fun to ride until your friends see you doing it.

Morning Wood: an erection a man has in the morning, usually as the body's way of preventing him from urinating in his sleep.

Morphophilia: a fetish for specific body shapes that deviate from the norm. This could include a love of fat people, dwarfs, amputees.

Moses: a man who enjoys going down on a woman during her period.

Mother Fucker: someone who is dumb, desperate, or dirty enough to have sex with his own mother.

Motorboat: rubbing your face between a woman's boobs while imitating the noise made by an outboard motor.

Mouth is Mightier than the Sword: a proverb that proclaims that a man's oral skills, both in his ability to charm and perform cunnilingus, do more to please a woman than a large penis.

Mowing the Backyard: shaving one's buttock.

Mpreg: "male pregnancy". This fantasy is

often reserved for the realms of hentai pornography.

MRS Degree: what a woman earns when she drops out of college to get married or to have a child.

MTF, M2F: "male-to-female."; a transsexual who was born a genetic male, but who has or is transitioning into a female.

Mud Flaps: large, hanging ass cheeks.

Mud Shark: a white woman who dates black men.

Mud Whistle: a noisy and filthy anus.

Muff Diver: A lesbian.

Muff Diving: cunnilingus.

Muff Teaser: finger, suck, eat, etc. a girl until she is begging for it. Then rub your stiffy round her golden valley until she screams at you to give her a banging. Right when her frustration is at its highest level, stop and finish with a DIY(do it yourself) hand job. Then leave the room without saying a word. Not to be tried if you want to shack up with the selfish lady again.

Muff: vagina.

Muffin Top: fat that spills over a person's pants, shorts, or skirt.

Multiple Body Parts: a fetish for sex partners with extra appendages, including breasts, orifices, penises, or limbs. Having multiple breasts may make a sex object seem hyper-female, just as multiple penises may make a male seem hyper masculine; related to monster fetishes.

Mumbler: an attractive person. So named as it is impossible to tell what such a person is saying as their beauty is too distracting.

Mummification: a type of bondage in which the submissive partner is completely immobilized, often by being wrapped in materials like plastic wrap or being stuffed in a body bag.

Munging: the one thing worse than genocide. One must first have no shame. Then he/she must use a newspaper to find the obituary of a recently deceased man or woman. Then must find a buddy, with no shame, who will aid them in this act. The partners then go to the cemetery where they dig up their victim, and flip a coin. The loser, (or winner depending on how sick you are), applies his/her lips to the genitals or anus of the corpse, while the other partner proceeds to climb the nearest tombstone and elbow drop the corpse's stomach. Thus forcing out a blend of rich bodily fluids and embalming materials onto the partners. This blend is called mung. The act of getting this blend on your face is called munging.

Municipal Cockwash: a promiscuous woman; slut.

Mushy Biscuit also known as limp biscuit: this is actually a very fun game. Just choose a piece of food that you and your male friends like to eat. Then you and your buddies form a tight circle around the food item and proceed to jerk off all over it. Last one to bust a nut gets the prize of eating the food.

Mysophilia: a fetish for dirt or filth; a fetish for smelling or tasting items stained by human fluids. Such items could include underwear, soiled clothes, or a used tampon.

Mystery Bus: the bus that seems to arrive at a bar when you are drunk, whisking away all the ugly patrons and replacing them with attractive people.

Mystery Taxi: the taxi that arrives in the morning after a night of heavy drinking and replaces the attractive person you brought home with the troll who is sleeping in your bed.

N

nachas: the buttocks , the ass; buttocks.

Nacho Salad: orgy. A delicious, messy indulgence that can only be fully enjoyed by a group.

Nacho: perineum; it is "not your" dick and "not your" asshole.

nackers: or; knackers / knacks , slang for; 1. The testicles. See penis for; 2. more rarely, the female breasts.

nacks: slang term for a woman's breasts. See breasts for and euphemisms; knick-knack, knick-knacking, knick-knacks.

nad bag: nad-sack, slang term for the scrotum, bags, ball basket, ball sack, ballock bag, bletherskate, bollock bag, bum bags, cable tie, debag, fart sack, nad bag, nad sack, nadds, scrotum, Silastic, two-bagger.

nadgers: nads / nadds , British slang term for the testicles, possibly a derivation of gonads; penis.

nafka: nafkeh; Yiddish and prior to that from the Aramaic nofka, meaning streetwalker prostitute.

nanophilia: sexual attraction for short desire to have sex with midgets, a fetish for midgets.

Narratophilia: a fetish for dirty talk, sex stories, or having conversations about sex.

Nasophilia: a fetish for noses. This includes an attraction to a specific type of nose or even a desire to penetrate a partner's nostrils.

NBR: "no beers required." a partner you would fuck without needing to be drunk.

Nebraskan Corn Cob: fucking a chick in the ass after she eaten a lot of corn. When you pull out and your dick is covered in corn, you have her eat the corn off your dick like it was corn on the cob.

Necro-beastiliality: sex with dead animals.

Necrophilia: a fetish for human corpses; sex with dead people.

needle-dick: a small penis.

New Jersey Meat-Hook: the unusual method of inserting one's finger in the ass of your partner while screwing her, and feeling her cervix. This procedure is most effective from behind.

New York Style Taco: anytime when you are so drunk that when you go down, you barf on her box. Happy trails.

New York Taco: a vagina that makes you nauseous while eating it due to a combination of the alcohol it took to desire this particular taco, the head movement required to ingest said taco, and the taste of fish that has been marinating in a humid environment all night.

Newcummer: a man who has recently come out publically about being gay.

Niddah: abstaining from sex 1/3 of the time to create sexual arousal the rest of the month.

Nipples: the pigmented and raised circles of skin at the center of breasts.

No Homo: a text-speak phrase intended to assert a male's heterosexuality following a statement that reveals his latent homosexuality. Ex. "If I was a chick, I would totally have Bieber-fever; No homo."

nob: 1. informal term for the head; 2. knob the penis or glans-penis; to have sex.

Non-Con: "non-consensual" BDSM play. this may refer to rape or sex play in which either partner is aroused by the fantasy of a forced encounter.

noogies: women's breasts.

Nookie: sex.

Nooner: a quickie that occurs during the middle of the day; lunch break, luncher.

Normophilia: a fetish for acts that do not violate laws, social norms, or religious doctrine.

Norwegian Torch blower: right before ejaculation you cover your penis in was and alcohol, set it on fire and jizz in her face.

novercaphobia: the fear of one's mother-in-law or step-mother.

Novice: a new comer to the fetish scene.

NSA: "no strings attached."; used in personals ads to indicate the user is looking for casual sex.

Nubile: a young, attractive woman who has just reached sexual maturity.

Nubs: small breasts.

Nullo: an extreme body modification fetish or paraphilia in which a person wants to have their genitals removed, or nullified. Similar to: amputation' amputee fetish, goro, vore, and orgasm denial.

Nut Huggers: tight pants worn by a man.

Nut Sack: scrotum.

Nuts: testicles.

Nyataimori: serving food, usually sushi, on a naked body.

Nyctophilia: a fetish for darkness or the night; scotophilia.

nymph : short for nymphomaniac.

Nymphomaniac: a woman with insatiable sexual desires;   psychologically addicted too, or dependent on, sex.; satyriasis, sex addict, uteromania.

O

Obscenity: what gives the judge, or the person deeming a thing obscene, an erection.

Objectum Sexuality, Objectophilia: a broad category of fetishes in which a person is sexually aroused by a specific class of physical objects like cars, monuments, or dolls.

Ochlophilia: a fetish for being in crowds.

Oculolinctus: a fetish for licking eyeballs.

Oculophilia: a partialism fetish that centers around the eyes.

Odaxelagnia: a fetish for biting.

Odontophilia: a fetish for teeth. This can manifest in a person liking to lick teeth, to leave bite marks, or to extract teeth.

O Face: the awkward face made while reaching orgasm.

An Old Fashion: a hand job.

Olfactophilia: a fetish for smells; involves body odors.

Omelet: an absurd sex act in which you ejaculate in your partner's ear, then fold it over.

One Hole too Many: a person who ruins her sex appeal by talking.

On the Blocks: a woman who is on her period. Like a car on the blocks, she is out of commission; Holy week.

One Night Stand: having sex with a person without the encounter being extended into a relationship.

Omega Male: a male who has so little power, or influence, that his selection of potential mates is severely limited; loser.

Onion: a person who becomes increasingly less appealing, and possibly worse smelling, the more layers of clothes she removes.

Open Relationship: a non-monogamous relationship.

Ophidicism: a fetish for reptiles.

Orchitis: inflammation of the testicles, which may be caused by a virus like mumps; didymalgia, testalgia.

Oregon Trail: the trail of hair that leads to a dense, wet forest of pubes. A sure sign a woman does not shave. A common feature of hippie women or butch lesbians; Amazon trail.

Orgasm: the climactic sensation that occurs at the height of sexual arousal.

Orgasm Denial: a type of fetish play in which a Dom teases the sub, but refuses to let him reach orgasm. This can include the use of such devices as a cock cage.

Orgy: group sex; bunch punch, club sandwich, crew screw, daisy chain, Fourgy, fuckathon, gang bang, group grope, nacho salad, run a train, team cream, three way

Osculate: 1. kiss; 2. to touch.

Osmolagnia: a fetish for body odors like sweat or flatulence.

Outercourse: dry humping or any form of non-penetrative sex;. sexual rubbing in which the participants are still clothed. Related to frottage and zipper sparks.

Oviposition: a fetish for egg laying. An uncommon kink, sometimes found in the furry community and usually only satisfied by means of fantasy or animation.

Ozolagnia: a fetish for strong smells.

Orgasm: the sexual climax.

Oculolinctus: licking your partner's eyeball for sexual pleasure.

Oyster: A derivation of the tea bag which is accomplished by numbing one's testicles with ice and then inserting them in a chicks mouth and letting the tramp munch on them.

P

Packing a Gun and a Holster: a hermaphrodite.

Padding: a fat fetish in which pleasure is derived from layering or stuffing one's clothes to simulate weight gain, either to oneself or a sexual partner; related to: fat fetish, feederism, feeding, feedism, gaining, inflation, immobility, stuffing.

Pansexual: someone who is open to any gender or most any kink when it comes to sex; trisexual.

Painal: painful anal sex.

Pain Play: a broad range of BDSM activities in which sexual pleasure is derived from inflicting or incurring pain.

Paint Brush: a wisp of pubic hair, usually on a woman; similar to a landing strip, but smaller.

Painted Lady: prostitute.

Panamanian Petting Zoo: when one forces one's partner to pick the nuts and corn out of a bowel movement. The partner then presents the nuts and corn to in a cup or a dish. One then tosses the nuts and corn onto the bed where the partner eats them like a goat or other typical petting zoo animal. " (Can be combined with the Kentucky Klondike Bar.)

Pasadena Mudslide: this happens when you leave a windy turd between the breasts of a woman while you straddle her neck for a blowjob;. related to a Cleveland Steamer.

Pattycake: while you're nailing some girl doggie style and your friend is catching some head off the same girl, you get a quick game of Pattycake going. This makes you reminisce of your childhood memories and eases the sight of watching your friend blow his load.

Paying The Rent: a position in which the woman is folded in half, knees above shoulders, while the man holds the back of her calves and bangs ferociously.

Paratrooping: hunting for a sexual partner in an effort to secure a place to sleep for the night; most often occurs when visiting a foreign city.

Paraphilia: any sexual fetish that is classified as a disorder because of its extreme nature, because it is harmful, or because it violates a society's mores or laws.

Pareunia: sex.

Parthenophilia: a fetish for virgins.

Partialism: a fetish for specific body parts. This includes such fetishes as nasophilia, oculophilia, and podophilia.

Parting the Red Sea: performing cunnilingus or having sex with a woman on her period. The saint who performs such an act is called, Moses; earning your red wings.

Pasadena Mudslide: an absurd sex act in which you defecate on your partner's chest while she performs oral sex on you in a reclining position. The excrement becomes a mudslide if it is runny or when it mixes with the pool of body fluid generated by oral sex.

Patty Cake: when the two guys in a devil's threesome high-five to prove they are not aroused by each other; often occurs when the two males make eye contact.

PAWG: "phat Ass white girl." A common porn category centered around thick white women who are often paired with black partners.

Paying the Rent: a form of prostitution in which sex is exchanged for goods or services, though the exchange is rarely explicit.

PDA: "public display of affection."; most often a crime of drunks and couples in the honeymoon phase of their relationship.

Peanut Butter and Jelly Sandwich: an absurd sex act in which a person defecates on a menstruating vagina.

Pearl Necklace: a piece of jewelry created when a man ejaculates on his partner's neck.

Pearl Tramp Stamp: when a man ejaculates on his partner's lower back.

Pediophilia: a fetish for sex toys, specifically dolls.

Pecattiphilia: a fetish for sinning, as defined by your religious upbringing; hamartophilia.

Pecker: penis.

Pecker Head: one who acts as though he thinks with his dick; dick head.

Pederast: a pedophile, particularly one who engages in anal sex with a boy.

Pedophile: one who engages in sexual acts with a child; pederast.

Pegging: when a woman uses a strap-on dildo to anally penetrate a man.

The Penguin: while performing fellatio, the woman walks out of the room before the act is complete, leaving the man with his pants around his ankles, waddling after her.

Penicorn: a mythical penis. Often refers to the dick of a man who exaggerates the size or nobility of his dick; an idealized penis with a vibrating, clitoral stimulator sticking off the shaft like a unicorn's horn.

Penis:

A: acorn, arrow, auger.

B: baby arm, baby maker, baloney pony, bean tosser, beaver cleaver, beef bayonet/hammer/stick, Big Ben, The Big Lebowski, Bilbo Baggings, bishop, black jack, blind salamander, boa, bone, bossman, bratwurst, burrito, bush beater.

C: captain, Chewbacca, choker, chub, cock, Conan the Barbarian, corn dog, corn holer, creamsicle, cream stick, Cupid's arrow, custard launcher, cyclops.

D: dagger, dick, dickie, dicktator, Dillinger, ding-a-ling, dingus, dink, dip stick, Dirty Harry, disco stick, dong, Don Juan, Donkey Kong, donut puncher, D train.

E: egg roll, enchilada, Excalibur.

F: family jewels, fiddle bow, fire hose, fishing rod, fish stick, foreman, frankfurter, French bread, fuck pole/stick/rod, funny bone.

G: Gary Coleman's forearm, gearstick, gear shift, giggle stick, Goliath, gravy maker, grower not a shower.

H: ham bone, Harry Johnson, Harry and the Hendersons, heat-seeking love missile, hitching post, hose, hot beef injector, hot dog, hung, hung like a horse, hung like a zebra.

I: Igor, inchworm.

J: jack-in-the-box, jaw breaker, Jimmy, Jimmy John, Jimmy Johnson, jizz whistle, Johnson, John Wang, joystick, junk.

K: kickstand, king dong, king kong, knob.

L: lap daschund, light saber, licorice stick, lincoln long, little head/soldier, lollypop, long john, love dart/gun/muscle/staff/stick/wand, louisville slugger.

M: magic stick, magic wand, man crank/horn/meat/, Mandingo, meat, meat loaf/popsicle/stick/troll, member, merrymaker, middle leg, milk man, miracle meat, missile launcher, Moby Dick, Mr. Bluevein, Mr. Fantastic, Mr. Goodbar, Mr. Goodwrench, Mr. Winky, mushroom head, mutton, my little pony, my other head.

N: nimrod, noodle.

O: the octagon, one-eyed monster/sailor/trouser trout/night crawler/wonder weasel/wonder worm.

P: package, pagan steeple, pecker, pee-pee, penicorn, peninsula, Percy, Peter, Peter Pan, pile driver, Pink Floyd, Pink Panther, pipe, pisser, piss pipe, pistole, piston, pocket piccolo, pocket rocket, pogo stick, poker, pole, pool stick, Popeye, pork sword, prick, pride & joy, private eye, prong, pump handle, purple-helmeted love warrior, pussy magnet, pweenis

R: the ramburglar, ram rod, raw meat, rod, rolling pin, rudder.

S: salami, sasquatch, sausage, scepter, semen truck, shaft, shamrock, shlong, short arm, skin chimney/flute, skunk ape, slut stick, snake, Spartacus, staff, staff sergeant, stick shift, St. Peter, summer sausage, sword.

T: tail spin, tally whacker, third leg, Titanic, tool, totem pole, trouser snake, tube steak, tuna can, Twinkie.

U,V,W,X,Y,Z: wand, wang, wedding tackle, weenie, weenus, wee-wee, weiner, wet willy, whacker, whistle, willy, Willy Wonka, Willy Wang, winky, yang, yogurt gun.

Other Mr. Bluevein, Mr. Fantastic, Mr. Goodbar, Mr. Goodwrench, Mr. Winky: Penis.

Peanut Butter And Jelly Sandwich: crap on a woman's snatch during menstruation.

Pearl necklace: when a guy ejaculates on the area below your neck and above your breasts.

Penis Elbow: any arm injury or soreness that results from masturbating or giving a handjob.

Penis Humiliation: a fetish for receiving derogatory comments about the size and inadequacies of your penis.

Penis Puffer: one who sucks enough dicks as to be addicted to the act.

Penis Pump: a cylindrical pump that creates a vacuum to draw blood into the member. Excessive use can cause serious vascular damage.

Penis: the male organ of sexual intercourse.

Penivore: one whose sexual diet consists entirely of devouring penises.

Peodeiktophilia: an exhibitionistic paraphilia in which a man is aroused by exposing his penis to unsuspecting victims.

Perineum: the area of skin between the balls and asshole, or the vagina and asshole; bridge, chode, gooch, grundle, nacho, taint.

Perineum: the skin and underlying tissue that lies between the vaginal opening and the anus or the scrotum and the anus.

Permaboner: a constant boner. Usually the result of a particularly arousing experience as opposed to the medical condition, priapism.

Personalities: breasts.

Perversion: any form of behavior that deviates from the social norm.

Pervert, Perv: someone with a fetish for deviant sexual behavior, as defined by the cultural context.

Pescatarian Fag: a heterosexual man who eats a lot of fish tacos but who can entice no women to gobble his sausage.

Pescatarian Porn: pornography that contains only melons and fish tacos, but no red meat.

Pet the Poodle: female masturbation.

Peter Pan: 1. an impotent penis, so named as it never wants to grow up; 2. an immature man who has the mentality of a boy.

Phallophilia: a fetish for large penises; macrogenitalism.

Pheromone: various chemicals animals secrete that influence the behavior of other members of the same species. These are often involved in attracting mates.

Philander: to engage in sexual affairs with a woman whom a man has no intention of marrying.

Philanderer: a man who seeks out sexual affairs with no intention of getting married.

Philemaphobia: a fear of kissing. Often stems from inexperience or a germ phobia.

Philter, Philtre: a love potion.

Phobophilia: a fetish for feeling afraid.

Phygephilia: a fetish for fugitives, or living as a fugitive; Hybristophilia.

Picasso Ass: when a woman wears too tight of panties or shorts, resulting in four distinct ass cheeks.

Pictophilia: a fetish for watching porn. Also, when one watches so much porn of the same act or person, he develops a fetish for that act or person.

Pig Roast: in a devil's threesome when a large woman is performing fellatio on one man and is penetrated by another; Chinese Finger Trap.

Pig Roast: while you're plugging some girl's hole doggie style, (up the dirt road or the funhole, pick your poison) she's blowing your best friend's cock at the same time, hence simulating a pig on a spit; .Chinese Finger Cuffs.

Pig Sticking: seeking out obese women to have sex with; hog hunting, whaling.

Pile Driver: a sex act in which the bottom partner balances her body atop her neck with her legs above her body. The man squats over her, angling himself down into her.

Pillow Biter: a gay man who receives anal sex.

Pillow Princess: a woman who enjoys receiving cunnilingus from men or women, but who does not reciprocate the act.

Pimp Check: informing a fuck buddy who starts to get attached, or who mistakes your situation for a relationship, that she has crossed a line.

Pimp: a prostitute's manager; aunt, hustler, mack, madame.

Pin the Tail On the Donkey: during a devil's threesome, the woman kneels doggy-style on the edge of the bed while wearing a blindfold or tucking her head under the bed sheets. The men take turns fingering, licking, or fucking her. This requires that the woman is more than comfortable with the idea of a threesome and that she trusts that neither man will play the guessing game, "Sheathed or unsheathed."

Pink Glove: hate when this happens. Every so often a girl is not wet enough during sex. When you finally pull out to give her money, the inside of her twat sticks to your hog. Thus, the pink glove.

Pink Posse: a group of gay friends.

Pink Sock: a flap of inverted colon that sometimes appears when a man pulls out too quickly during anal sex.

Pink Taco: like a fish taco, but without the fishy taste.

Pinup, Pin-Up: a photo or glossy magazine picture of an arousing woman mean to be hung up for admiration; often refers to a style of photography and burlesque that evokes the original pinup girls that were popularized during WWII; Bombshell.

Piquerism, Picquerism: a fetish for piercing, or penetrating, another person's skin. People with this fetish often concentrate on piercing erogenous zones.

Pirate Treasure: feces that appears during anal sex, particularly when it contains golden nuggets of corn.

Piss: 1. the act of urinating; 2. Urine; 3. a state of anger comparable to that of being urinated on, as in, "I am pissed at that ass clown."

Pit Job: when a man masturbates himself in another person's armpit.

Pitch a Tent: to get an erection.

Pitcher: the partner delivering the penis to home plate during anal sex between two men. The top. The counterpart to a "catcher."

Pity Fuck: sex performed out of a sense of charity.

Plating: defecating on a clear plate positioned over a person's face; Similar to a glass bottom boat and a hot lunch.

Plating: take a clear, glass plate and place it on

your partners face, then crap on it. It gives them a nice view without all the messy cleanup.

Play Action Fake: any move that tricks a woman into thinking that the man has climaxed in order for him to unsuspectingly ejaculate on her face; often involves spit.

Play Chopsticks: when two guys masturbate together, creating their own kind of simple, yet beautiful duet.

Player: a person who approaches seduction as a game.

Playing Hard to Get: a mating strategy in which a person artificially enhances her perceived social value by pretending to be uninterested in a pursuer, thus forcing the interested party to work for her affection. This ritual also allows the pursuer to demonstrate his social value by overcoming this resistance.

Playing the Skin Flute: giving a blowjob with particular grace, rhythm, and light fingering.

Pliant: flexible in body, or in mind, in relation to what a person will do in bed.

Plow: sex.

Plumper: fatty.

Plushies: having ursusagalmatophilia; furries.

Plushofilia: teddy bear fetish

Plushophilia: fetish for stuffed animals. ursusagalmatophilia.

PNP: "party n play." used in personal ads to express a desire to do drugs, usually methamphetamines, during sex.

Pocket Pool: male masturbation.

Podophilia: a partialism fetish that revolves around feet.

Poke: sex.

Pole Smoker: someone who is addicted to performing fellatio; penis puffer.

Polyiterophilia: a fetish for group sex.

Polyphallic: characterized by many phalluses; often used in reference to art or sex toys.

Poofter: a gay man.

Poon, Poonani, Poonany, Poontang: vagina.

Poontang Plantation: brothel.

Pop the Cherry: taking a woman's virginity.

Popcorn Trick: first, take your girlfriend to the cinemas, for a nice romantic date. Buy a tub of popcorn, wait until the lights dim, and carefully make a hole in the bottom on the tub. Then, inconspicuously insert your penis through the bottom of the tub into the popcorn and casually offer some to your lady. When she digs in, she will find nice surprise.

Popcorning: during a movie date, the man unsuspectingly pokes a hole in the bottom of the popcorn bag or bucket. He inserts his dick into the hole and waits for his date to discover the buttery treat.

Popinjay: a braggart who excessively peacocks himself in an attempt to attract sex partners.

Poppers: alkyl nitrites inhaled as recreational drugs, often to relax the anal sphincter prior to anal sex.

Popple: a young, attractive woman with a cute face who carries some extra weight, but who is still young enough that her fat is not offensive or marked with cellulite. Such women are prized because you can cuddle with them or roll them into a ball and bounce them about roughly without injuring them physically or psychologically.

Porking: sex with a partner who is large enough to be a farm animal.

Porky Piggin; the female who has received the Alabama Hot Pocket. In Alabama, you see, good old redneck boys, when bored, would fuck pig troughs or large, wet piles of mud. To properly perform the Porky Piggin' follow-up procedure, one must take a massive shit onto the vagina without spreading the lips. This creates a core that enters the woman, and then dregs that explode out all over her. By randomly stabbing with the cock, one will successfully Porky Piggin' the girl–repeating, naturally, the action that would normally be associated with screwing a pile of mud or animal trough.

Porn Storm: pop-up windows that bombard a computer screen while the user is searching for free porn.

Pornocchio: a person who lies about his porn watching habits.

Pornstache: a creepy mustache attributed to male porn performers in the 1970s.

Possum: a sex partner who just lies there, as if dead, during sex; intercorpse.

Postage Slot: a vagina that looks like a slit in the skin with none of the labia minora showing.

Pound: sex.

Pregnancy Fetish: a common fetish for fertile woman who are visibly pregnant. This fantasy often focuses on swollen breasts and bellies. Related to impregnation fetish.

Pregnant, Preggers, Prego: baby bound, belly up, in trouble, knocked up, loaded, one in the oven, pea in the pod, preggers, preggy, preggo, swallowed a watermelon seed, with child.

Premarital Sex: when religious people have sex before they are married a first time.

Premature Ejaculation: a sexual dysfunction in when a man climaxes shortly before or after achieving penetration.

Premature Evacuation: sneaking away in the wake of a one night stand.

Prepuce: the skin surrounding and protecting the head of the penis or the clitoris; foreskin.

Priapism: a painful medical condition in which the penis remains erect in the absence of sexual arousal; permaboner.

Prick Peddler/Pusher: gigolo.

Prick: 1. Penis; 2. a dick head

Pricknic: An orgy of gay men.

Privates, Private Parts: genitals.

Procrasterbating: wanting to masturbate but waiting to do it another time; procrastinating via masturbating.

Promiscuous: possessing a liberal understanding of sexuality.

Prophylactic: a device or measure used to prevent the transmission of disease; refers to a condom.

Prostiboots: boots that a streetwalker would wear.

Prostitute: one who accepts money in exchange for sexual favors; bachelor's wife, call girl, company girl, courtesan, floosie, harlot, harpie, hooker, hoose bag, hustler, lady of the night, lizard lot, mattress, painted lady, pavement princess, sister of mercy, sporting girl, streetwalker, strumpet, tail, tart, vent renter, whore, window tapper, working girl.

Psychrocism: a fetish for being cold, or being with a partner who is cold; a fetish for cold objects such as snow, ice, or a frozen glass dildo.

Pubephilia: a fetish for pubic hair.

Pubes, Pubic hair: secondary hair that grows around human sex organs.

Pudding Pop: a penis after dirty anal sex.

Pudendum: the external genital organs, especially those of a woman.

Puerto Rican Fog Bank: while 69ing with your partner, release a cloud of sphincter fog directly into her nostrils.

Pug Noshing: noisy and aggressive cunnilingus, comparable to the way a pug attacks a food bowl.

Pull the Goalie: to stop using various forms of birth control, usually in attempt to conceive a child.

Puma: a woman who is younger than a cougar, or who is not a MILF, but who still preys on younger men.

Punch Drunk Love: intense feelings of lust that interfere with your ability to think rationally.

Puppet Show: a hand job that involves the giver telling a dirty story. A handjob given while watching a porno or while in a movie theater. A handjob performed while the giver talks about nonsexual things, such as describing her day or chatting on the phone with someone else.

Purple Mushroom: created when an erect penis is pressed so hard into the inside of a person's cheek during fellatio, that the outer skin creates a purple protrusion.

Purple Mushroom: this occurs when a woman is giving you oral sex and you withdraw your penis in order to poke it back into her cheek. It should leave a lasting impression.

Pushing Rope: attempting to penetrate an orifice with a semi-erect or limp penis.

Pussy Broom: mustache.

Pussy Licking: cunnilingus.

Pussy Magnet: 1. a man or object that naturally attracts positive, female attention; 2. Penis.

Pussy Whipped: when a man's actions are controlled by the prospect of sex with a particular woman.

Pussy: 1. Vagina; 2. a man who is timid or scared.

Put Out: sex.

Pweenis: a tiny penis; weenis.

Pygmalionism: a fetish for a statue or a human-like image, especially a work that is of one's own creation; involves rubbing oneself against a statue; agalmatophilia; Pygmalio, in

Greek mythology, who falls in love with an idealized image of a woman he carves out of ivory.

Pygophilia: a fetish for butts, specifically seeing, touching, or playing with a butt.

Pyrolagnia: a fetish for watching or setting fires.

Pyrophilia: a fetish for using fire or burning objects in sex play.

The Princeton Rub: when two men rubs their penises together in a sexual manner; cock rub, bumping dicks, frictation, frontism, frot, the Ivy League rub, knocking cocks, Oxford style, the Princeton Rub, sword fighting, tummy sticks.

Q

Quabbing a Twab: when you are having sex with a seal and the seal poops out a baby seal, so you hit it with a shovel. Then, you his the mother in the head with a shovel for being such a dumb seal, and continue to bone her. When you are done boning her then you poop on her.

Quarterbacking: when defecating in a filthy toilet, one squats above the seat; the person holding such a pose looks like a quarterback waiting for the snap.

Quatro Train: a foursome; riding the quarto train.

Queef Greased: the materials spewed out at lightning speed as a result of a vaginal fart. The material is often quite unpleasant and probably even toxic. Some are turned off of this while others find it a pleasant fetish.

Queef: a well known, but sometimes embarrassing occurrence. Queefing happens when air gets trapped in a girls vagina, and makes a soft hissing, or farting kind of a sound while that air is released; the noise that occurs when air that is trapped in the vagina rushes out, often during sex or soon after.

Queen: a diva or a gay man who must have everything his way, and who is overly dramatic. The gay equivalent to calling a woman a princess.

Queening: sitting on a face as if it is a royal throne.

Queer as a Three Dollar Bill: a flamboyant homosexual.

Queer Bait: a heterosexual who is often mistaken for a homosexual.

Queer Goggles: when alcohol allows a person to act on his or her homosexual desires without fear of the social stigmas that normally constrain such actions; beer goggles.

Queer Hole: a man's asshole.

Queer: a homosexual.

Quick Lube: a quickie, particularly during lunch time. Non romantic sex needed to help one work more efficiently; nooner, lunch break

Quickie: a sexual encounter that is short lived, often due to time constraints or to avoid detection.

Quim: vagina.

Quinny: a rather Victorian term for a pussy/vagina.

R

Racing Stripe: a line of pubic hair extending up from the top of the vagina; Brazilian, landing strip; paintbrush.

Rack: breasts.

Raging-Semi: that erection a guy starts getting before he can no longer control his urge to get relieved.

Rainbow Kiss: 1. when a guy eats a girl out while she is having her period then kisses her and spits some of the blood back into her mouth; 2. cunnilingus while a woman is on her period; earning your red wings, parting the red sea.

Raincoat: condom; goulashes, slicker.

Rake: one who is considered immoral, particularly due to his sexual lifestyle; Debauchee, libertine, rake, roué.

Ram: sex; when attacking from behind, you start ramming her head against the wall in a rhythmic motion. The force of the wall should allow for deeper penetration. Very handy in those lulls in penile sensitivity.

Randy: horny.

Raptophilia: being sexually aroused by the fantasy of raping another; Biastophilia.

Raw Jaw: a person who is known for performing oral sex; mighty mouth.

Ray-Bans: when testicles are draped over a person's eyes to provide complete protection from the sun and to make a fashion statement; Arabian goggles.

Rear Admiral: 1. an absurd sex act in which the man mounts his partner doggy style, then yanks back her arms and pushes her face first around the floor as though he is captaining a small vessel; 2. a gay man.

Red Wings: a mark of distinction earned after performing cunnilingus on a woman who is menstruating; another name for navigating the moose knuckle with your tongue while discovering the girl is on her rag. Be a real man and earn your red wings soldier.

Resuscitation: when a girl is asleep, carefully open her mouth so that she doesn't awake. Then, squat over her face and carefully place your turd hole on her lips. When the time is right, you let rip the biggest baddest fart ever known to man and see if it wakes her up. Great fun during those long sleepless nights.

Retifism: a foot fetish that revolves around shoes; altocalciphilia.

Reverse Cowgirl: a sex position in which the woman rides atop the man while facing away from him.

Reverse Missionary: doggy-style in which the woman lies on her stomach.

Reverse Swallow: when an anus ingests something, such as a condom or a sex toy lacking a flared base; requires a medical team to extract the object.

Rhabdophilia: a fetish for being beaten, flogged, or whipped.

Rhythm Method: instead of using birth control or contraceptives, some religious people try to avoid pregnancy by only having sex at certain times of the woman's menstrual cycle; Vatican Roulette.

Rim Job: when you put your legs over your head and someone licks your asshole; tonguing right around someone's asshole and vagina.

Rimmadonna: someone who enjoys giving or receiving rim jobs.

Rimming, Rim Job: analingus.

Ring the (Back) Doorbell: when a man taps or gently presses the head of his penis against his partner's anal sphincter, either to see if she is open for anal sex, or simply to help relax the anal muscles.

Road Head: oral sex performed on the driver of a moving vehicle; meal on wheels.

Robotism, Robot Fetish: a fetish for robots, particularly using robots in sex play. This fetish may become more common with the rise of increasingly automated sex dolls.

Rod Rash: chaffing on the shaft of the penis from overuse.

Rod: penis.

Rodeo: similar to the Bronco. You start once again, banging a chick from behind. At a pre-arranged time you grab her hair with one hand just as several buddies bust into the room. See if you can hang on for 8 seconds cowboy.

Rodeo: when penetrating a partner from behind, the man does any number of things that will cause his partner to try and buck him off. The man attempts to maintain penetration with one hand around his partner's waist and the other in the air. The instigating event can be anything from the man claiming he has an STD to his friends bursting in the room; The Bronco.

Rolling Dutch Oven: when a driver farts in a hot car and flips on the child safety locks to prevent his passengers from rolling down the windows to escape the smell.

Roman Helmet: when a limp dick and balls is draped over a person's face, creating a war helmet.

Roman shower: 1. Vomit; vomiting on someone to heighten sexual arousal.

Roué: a rogue devoted to a life of pleasure and vice; debauchee, libertine, rake.

Rough Sex: often inflicting some physical harm for a sexual thrill.

#1 Scream and yell. Not all of us are sexual screamers. But when you get roughed up and shed your vocal inhibitions, you'd feel more relaxed and carefree, which will make you wilder.

#2 Nibble and bite. Using teeth is always a great way to bring out the animal in you when you're in bed. Bite hard, but not hard enough to draw blood. Focus on erogenous zones like the neck, the breasts, belly, inner thighs and around the elbows and ankles.

#3 Claw your lover. Scratch with your fingernails. Literally. Running a painful line with your fingernails against the soft skin of your lover's back will send a sexy rush that can cause a lot of pain too. But when you're on a sexual high, all that pain will turn to sexual adrenalin.

#4 Pull each other's hair. Grab a handful of your lover's hair just above the scalp at the back of the head, and tug at it. You won't lose your grip and yet, the pain will feel more pleasurable than when you hold your lover by the lower ends of their hair.

#5 Aggressive movements. Pound each other like there's no tomorrow, and the aggressive to-and-fro movements will turn both of you on, just as long as both of you can hold on long enough. But remember, you're dealing with fragile body parts here, so don't get carried away and push too deep or too hard.

#6 The burning slap. Slap each other across the face or the chest, or if you're standing behind your partner who's on all fours, slap their back or their butt. The searing pain will bring out the animal in your lover.

#7 Asphyxiation. For many kinky lovers, cutting off the oxygen supply to the brain arouses them to an all time high. But be very careful here, as you could end up hurting your lover while choking or throttling them. Instead of trying to choke your lover, just place your hands gently on your lover's neck and massage it just until they feel your pressure. Don't try blocking the oxygen supply completely, you definitely should leave that to the professional kinky chokers who know what they're doing. Another alternative is smothering the face, either by gently using your palms without too much force or by placing a porous pillow over your lover's mouth.

#8 Abusive words. Ever heard the lines, "say my name!"☐ or "call me a bitch!"☐? Well, many lovers love getting called trashy names and hearing dirty abuses. If your lover's into being called a whore, go ahead and indulge them.

#9 Fantasizing and role play. The words you choose play a big part in setting the mood for rough sex. Grab your partner by their hair as you lay on their side, and whisper something dirty about what you intend to do to them. Or pretend like both of you are two other people, like two strangers on a flight, or drunken strangers at a party. If you have an active imagination, you'd get your lover in the mood even before doing anything else.

#10 Force. Forcing your partner to perform sexual acts can work quite well if both of you enjoy dominant and submissive roles. Force their head down on you, or hold your lover by their neck or hands and order them around in bed.

#11 Whips. If your fingernails aren't painful enough, use short whips. They hurt more, and it's a lot more dominating and insulting to be whipped.

#12 Tie your lover up. Tie your lover's hands and legs to the bedpost or hold their hands firmly with your own hands. The helplessness of the situation could turn both of you on, because one of you will be in complete control of the other person. You could also use cuffs instead of ropes.

#13 Spanking. Spanking is the poster boy of rough sex. When someone thinks of rough sex, almost always they visualize a hard smack on a bare bottom. You know to smack, so go right ahead and smack them until they turn deep red.

#14 Force yourself on your lover. The rape fantasy. If your partner gets aroused by the thought of being sexually overpowered by a stranger, talk dirty about a fantasy where your lover's being forced into sexual submission by someone else. And as you visualize the scene, make sure your hands continue to play rough with your partner's body.

#15 Toys and gags. Rough toys and gags are not for the fainthearted. But if you want to take that road into rough sex, go right on. It may not be for everyone, but if you do enjoy extreme rough sex, perhaps bdsm is the way to go.

Rub One Out: masturbation.

Rubber Fuckie: a waterproof vibrator used during long baths. Some are actually shaped like rubber duckies .

Rubber: condom.

Rubenesque: the word chubby chasers use to describe the objects of their affection.

Rufies Rohypnol, R-2: the date rape drug some vile ass clowns drop in women's drinks, as such boys clearly have no redeeming qualities that would make a woman want to willingly have sex with them.

Rump Raid: anal sex.

Rusty Trombone: Licking a man's asshole while simultaneously giving him a hand job: This is what happens when you've got a less then respectable female (AKA be-yatch) tongue deep in your chute:)description—She wiggles her tongue as she does the reach around to pump you like a Catholic priest doing an Altar Boy, thus mimicking a trombone player.

Ruttish: characterized by excessive sexual desire; lascivious, libidinous, lustful, salacious.

Rowdy Roddy Pipper: while penetrating his partner from behind, the man puts his partner in a full nelson or any type of choke-hold.

S

Saddle Up: the initial act of anal sex.

Saddlebacking: when two straight teenagers, endeavoring to preserve an evangelical girl's virginity, engage in unprotected, anal intercourse.

Sadism: a fetish for dominating a submissive partner by inflicting physical, emotional, or psychological abuse; the desire or need to inflict pain or humiliation on others to enhance sexual arousal.

Sadist: a person who is sexually aroused by administering pain to himself or others.

Sadomasochism, SNM, S&M: a broad category of activities in which one partner derives sexual pleasure from administering or receiving psychological or physical pain.

Safe Word: a word or phrase that is uttered during fetishistic play to stop the action, particularly when the play becomes too painful or intense.

Salacious: characterized by devious sexual desires or behaviors; indecent, lascivious, lecherous, lewd, lustful, prurient, scabrous, salacious.

Salami: penis.

Saline Balls: fetish play in which the scrotum is infused with a saline solution from an IV to make the testicles appear gigantic. The process takes around an hour, and the inflation lasts for a few days until the solution is fully absorbed into the body. The medical term is, scrotal inflation.

Salirophilia: a fetish for soiling the objects of one's desire. This often manifests in a sex partner being coated in filth; related to bukkake, urolagnia or coprophilia.

Sandwich: when a woman is pressed between two men while being penetrated anally and vaginally; DP.

Santorum: the frothy mixture of lube and fecal matter that is sometimes the by-product of anal sex.

Sapiosexual: attracted to intelligent people.

Sascrotch: the hairy crotch of a male or female that looks and smells as though it resides in the swamp.

Satyriasis: 1. a male's uncontrollable sexual desires; 2. a neurotic condition in which men have sex with as many people as possible; gynecomania, nymphomania.

Sauce Shelf: breasts. cleavage.

Sausage Party, Sausage Fest: a gathering in which there are far more men than women.

Sausage Sandwich: masturbating a penis between a woman's breasts.

Scabrous: sexually scandalous.

Scat: Shit.

Scatophilia: a fetish for excrement; the desire to cover yourself and even eat shit; eating your own or someone else's shit as a sexual turn-on.

Schlong: penis.

Scissoring, Scissor Fight: when two women

intertwine legs and rub their vaginas together.

Scopophilia: 1. a fetish for being a voyeur; 2. an exhibitionistic fetish for watching a partner or yourself engage in sexual activity. May involve mirrors or a sex tape; Mixophilia.

Score: sex.

Scoregasm: yelling, screaming, moaning, grunting etc. associated with a particular team scoring during a game, especially after a tense moment of the game; often done unintentionally with exercise equipment sold on an infomercial; thigh master, shake weight, fitness ace power.

Scotophilia: A fetish for darkness or the night; nyctophilia.

Screw: sex.

Screwicorn: when (mostly) a lesbian puts her strap-on dildo on her forehead and proceeds to go at her partner like a crazed unicorn.

Scrotum, Srote: the pouch of skin covering the testicles; ball bag, ball sack, nut sack, sack; the pouch of loose skin that contains the testes.

Scumbag: 1. a used condom; 2. a person whose

value is comparable to that of a used condom.

Seduce: to purposefully entice another person to have sex.

Seducer, Seductress: one who seduces.

Seduction: the art of enticing someone to do what they secretly want to do—namely sex.

Semen Sneeze: a sneeze that occurs during fellatio or after swallowing semen. A true semen sneeze ejects semen from the nose or mouth.

Semen, Seminal Fluid: the pasty, white goop ejaculated from the penis, containing spermatozoa; baby juice, bull gravy, buttermilk, cream, cum, dick juice, dick milk, ejaculate, glue, gravy, honey, hot milk, jam, jelly, jism, jizz, juice, load, love liquor, man oil, marrow, ointment, pudding, scum, seed, skeet, slime, soap, sperm, splooge, spume, spunk, swimmers, tallow, wad, white honey, yogurt; the whitish fluid that constitutes the ejaculate, consisting of sperm and secretions from the seminal vesicles, prostate, and Cowper's glands.

Semi: a semi-erection.

Semi-detached: a couple that separated but still has frequent sex.

Sensualist: one devoted to sensations or the pursuit of carnal pleasures; apolaustic, hedonist, sensualist, sybarite.

Seventy-One, 71: a 69 but with a finger stuck in each other's ass.

Sex Machine: 1. one who is as efficient as the energizer bunny when it comes to sex; 2. a mechanized sex toy often used exclusively for penetration. Many of these machines are homemade; drilldo.

Sex: engaging in physical contact where body parts are inserted into a partner and orgasm is achieved; the physical act of procreation; physical pleasure.

A: action, ass.

B: ball, bag, bang, bash the beaver, beat cakes/cheeks, beat the rug, beef injection, be intimate, belly ride, bisect the triangle, blanket drill, boing, boink, bone, bonk, breed, bump nasties, bump, bumper cars, bump uglies, bury the bone/weasel, bush patrol, butte the biscuit.

C: carnal knowledge, coitus, consummate, copulation, couple up.

D: dance the mattress jig, dick diving, dicking, diddle, dip the wick, do it, disappearing cane trick, do the deed, do the funky chicken, do the laundry, do the nasty.

E:

F: feed the kitten, fiddle, fix her plumbing, flesh session, fog the windows, fornicate, four-legged frolic, freak, fuck.

G: get a piece, get biblical, get into her pants, get it on, get laid, get lucky, get one's noodle wet, get an oil change, get physical, get some, get some ass, get your dick wet, get your pole polished, give it up, go all the way, go at it, go to bed with, go to the bone yard, go to town, greet and meat, grind, grind one's tool.

H: hanky panky, have relations, hide the ferret/Nazi/salami, hit it, hit skins, horizontal mambo, horizontal tango, hump.

I: intercourse.

J: jackhammer, joined at the groin, joy ride, jump your bones.

K: kicking the tires, knock boots,

L: lay, lay pipe, lie with, lock crotches, love.

M: make babies/it/love/whoopee, make sexy time, mate, mess around, mingle limbs, mount.

N: nail, nooky, nookie,

P: park your yacht in hair harbor, peg, piece of ass, piece of tail, pin, plow, plug, poke, polish your pole, pork, pound, pump.

Q:

R: rail, ram, ride, ride the flagpole, roll in the hay, romp.

S: sexual congress, sexual relation, score, screw, shack up, shag, sink the sausage, slay, sleep with, slide into home, spelunking, squat jumps in the cucumber patch, squatting on the hog, stable my stallion, stuff.

T: tap that ass, thread the needle, tumble.

U:
V:
W:
X,Y,Z:

Sexcellence: sexual excellence.

Sexercism: having sex with a new partner in order to remove the demon of guilt and the emotional baggage leftover from the horrible death of a previous relationship.

Sexomnia: like sleepwalking, but instead of taking a stroll the sleeping person has sex; Somnophilia.

Sexpert: a particularly annoying person who,

for whatever reason, believes she is an expert when it comes to sex.

Sex-reassignment surgery, SRS: the reconstruct of a person's genitals to more accurately reflex the sex they identify with; Bottom Surgery.

Sextasy: 1. the state one achieves right after fulfilling a sexual fantasy; 2. taking the drugs, Viagra and ecstasy, simultaneously.

Sexting: sending sexual text messages or images electronically.

Shaft: penis.

Shag: sex.

Shagable: fuckable; attractive.

Shagbag: a promiscuous female or gay man. A receptacle for sex.

Shame Shower: a shower to remove the physical and emotional remnants of a filthy and regrettable sexual experience.

Shark Fin: the impression of a woman's vagina as seen through her swimming suit or wet suit.

Shark Week: during a devil's threesome, one man lies on a bed with his head at the edge of the mattress. The woman then lies on him in the 69 position. The second man mounts her from behind in a standing doggy-style position. This move mimics the feeding frenzy and uninhibited orgy that occurs after sharks converge on a whale carcass. It also brings the standing man dangerously close to having his dick chomped by the bottom man. Anal sex will reduce the risk of the top man's balls slapping the bottom man's forehead, but it increases the risk of santorum dripping on the bottom man's forehead.

Shart: a hybrid between shitting and farting.

Sheila: chick. Woman; Australian for a woman.

She-Male: a pre-op, MTF transsexual.

Shirley Temple: when any type of clear soda is poured in a menstruating vagina during cunnilingus.

Shit Canned: fired.

Shit Dick: 1. a penis coated in santorum after anal sex; 2. a dirty fucker.

Shit Faced: so drunk that you could have shit on your face and would not notice.

Shit Head, Shit for Brains: anyone who behaves as though his brain is composed of fecal matter.

Shit Hole: 1. an asshole, in both senses of the word' shit ass, shit bag, shit bagger, shit pipe, shit spitter, shit stain; 2. a low quality place or dwelling.

Shit House: bathroom.

Shit: feces. the second most popular American curse word after fuck.

Shitty: a situation that is as unsavory as dealing with a pile of excrement.

Shocker: inserting your pointer and middle finger in a woman's vagina while sliding a pinky in her ass; two in the pink and one in the stink.

Shop Vac: a mouth that is capable of slurping up a wide variety of penises; a mouth that can simultaneously accommodate a dick and balls.

Short and Curlies: pubic hair.

Short Eyes: a term signifying a child, or underage rapist; also a prison term inmates have an excuse to murder a child rapist; the idea that child abuse leads one into criminality and the child abuser who ends up in jail is fair game to the once-abused.

Shrimping: sucking or licking toes; a guy who sexes you, ejaculates and then sucks the cum out of your ass with a straw.

Side Boob: when the side of a boob is exposed in a revealing outfit.

Siderodromophilia: a fetish for trains. Often involves having sex while on a train.

Sideways Smile: 1. ass crack; 2. vagina.

Significant Other, SO: a politically correct term used to refer to a sexual or romantic partner, including a boyfriend, girlfriend, wife, or husband.

Simba, The Lion King: when a man anoints a person's forehead with his semen, then smears it across her face with his penis.

Sin Hole: a vagina, particularly one belonging to a woman who believes premarital sex or carnal pleasure is evil.

Sitophilia: a fetish for food. Often involves incorporating food into sexual foreplay.

Sixty-Eight, 68: when one partner receives oral sex without returning the favor. He owes her one.

Sixty-Nine, 69: a sex position that allows for both partners to simultaneously give and receive oral sex; doubleheader, flip-flop, head over heels, loop de loop.

Size Queen: one who is obsessed with penis

size, to the point where this is a main criteria for having sex with, or dating, a man.

Skank: a promiscuous woman.

Skeet: semen.

Ski Poles: during a devil's threesome, the woman simultaneously pumps both men's erections with her hands.

Skid Marks: shit stains left on underwear, or on bed sheets during sex; racing stripes.

Skiing: while facing in the same direction, a girl gets between two guys and jerks them both off, thus imitating some hardcore cross-country action.

Skull Fuck: rough or forced fellatio; a threat to use an enemy's corpse for sexual gratification.

Skuntch: a skanky cunt.

Slap The Banana: masturbate.

Slave: a submissive partner who has an ongoing relationship with a dominant master.

Slhore: a slutty whore; slunt.

Slime Fetish: a fetish for slimy substances, which often takes the form of tentacles;

related to wet and messy fetishes, and sploshing; goo fetish.

Slob on the Knob: fellatio.

Slore: a slut/whore.

Slot B: asshole.

Slumming: engaging in a relationship or having sex with someone below one's social class.

Slump Buster: a sex partner whose primary purpose is to end an extended period without sex; when a professional athlete finds the dirtiest, nastiest, fattest, most disease-ridden skank and puts the wood to her with the intent that it will break up a slump.

Slump: an extended period without sex; a Dry Spell.

Slunt: a slutty cunt. Similar: slhore.

Slurry Bucket: a vagina or anus large enough to accommodate a hand.

Slut Shaming: the cultural practice of characterizing promiscuous females as evil or morally corrupt in order to discourage women from being as sexually forward as males.

Slut: the most popular American term for a

promiscuous woman; adultera, alley cat, bangster, bed bunny, bimbo, bitch, cum dumpster, cum guzzler, cum slut, cum tart, eager beaver, floozie, hobby horse, ho, hoe, ho bag, hoozie, hooze bag, hussy, loose, nympho, meat hound, sexpot, skank, slore, slot job, slut bag, stray, tramp.

SMD: "Suck my dick."; often used as an insult in text-speak.

Smegma: a mixture of shed skin cells, body oil, body fluids and various other funky material that accumulates under the foreskin of an uncircumcised penis, and in the folds of the labia minora.

Smexy: smart and sexy.

Snail Trail: the glistening trail of dried semen that often appears inside a man's underwear after he becomes aroused or ejaculates. The trail resembles the silvery tracks left by a snail.

Snape: Snuggle rape; when one person snuggles an unwilling or unconscious partner.

Snatch: vagina given to pocketing items, like penises or semen.

Sneezing Fetish: a fetish for watching others sneeze, usually while naked. This may be related to the fact that sneezing is involuntary and cannot be faked, as well as the fact that sneezing triggers some of the same nerves as an orgasm; related to tickling.

Snerd Nurgling: the act of moving your anal lovers turds about within his/her lower intestine with your dick. Really popular with the lavender boys.

Snoodling: when an uncircumcised gay man pulls his extra foreskin over the dick of another gay man and proceeds to jerk him off. These guys have way too much free time. Can be used at as a great derogatory term as in, "You Snoodler".

Snow Balling: spitting semen from one mouth to another. May occur a number of times; when a girl gives head with ice cream in her mouth.

Snuff: A paraphilia that centers around the fantasy of killing or being killed. Related to: amputation/amputee fetish, body modification fetish, goro, medical fetish, nollo, non-con, pain play, vore, necrophilia.

Snuggle: to hold or embrace; cuddle, croodle.

SO: "Sex offender."; used in prison to designate a certain class of offender. Similar to: kidmo.

Sodomite: one who participates in sexual acts, particularly anal sex, that are considered deviant by the surrounding culture. : brown hatter, bugger, bum fucker, butt fucker, corn holer, gut butcher, gut fucker, gut scratcher, gut stuffer, shit stirrer, stern chaser, stuffer, turd burglar.

Solicitation: the act of selling or seeking sex for money; yard sale.

Somnophilia: a   fetish   for   asleep   or unconscious sex partners; sleeping princess syndrome.

Sounding: the act of inserting something into the urethra to inflict a mixture or pleasure and pain; the medical practice of removing blockage and clearing up urination issues; using medical grade sounding rods made of steel. Sounding enthusiasts have branched out, using a variety of objects, including such seemingly painful and harmful objects and toothbrushes or glass; urethra play.

Soup Kitchen: a hobo orgy, often performed in a confined space.

Space Docking: when an uncircumcised man wraps his foreskin around a partner's penis. So named as the connection resembles the docking of space stations.

Spank the Monkey: Male masturbation. to jack off; spankin, wankin, beatin: masturbating; when one gives sexual pleasure to oneself; spooning: usually when a male enters a woman from behind while both are lying on their sides.

Special Purpose: penis.

Spectrophilia: a fetish involving the fantasy of having sex with ghosts.

Sperm Dumptser: some place to put the stuff that comes out of your junk.

Spider Webbing: when semen shoots from an ass after anal sex.

Spiderman: an absurd sex act in which a man ejaculates in his hand then flings the semen at his partner.

Spill one's Seed: 1. sex; 2. to ejaculate.

Spinner: a petite woman who could easily be spun around a dick during sex. This especially refers to small strippers who can twirl around the pole with ease.

Spit Fuck: sex using only saliva as lubricant.

Spit Game: A blatant attempt at verbal seduction.

Spit Roast: a threesome sex act in which the bottom partner is being penetrated from behind by one man while performing fellatio on another man; hog roast.

Splooge: semen.

Sploshing: splashing watery foods on one's self or a partner as an act of foreplay or for sexual gratification.

Spooge: semen.

Spread Eagle: when a person's legs are spread, forming a V shape.

Spunk Bucket: 1. slut. 2. vagina. 3. Asshole.

Spunk: semen.

Squashing: a fetish for being squashed by another partner.

Squirt: when a female ejaculates.

Squirter: a woman who ejaculates.

Stag Party: a guys night or bachelor's party. These gatherings exclude wives and girlfriends, but often includes strippers, prostitutes, and/or promiscuous women.

Starfish Trooper: one who enjoys licking the assholes of those who have never engaged in anal play; refers to a gay man; asstronaut.

Starfish: Asshole; chocolate starfish.

STD, STI: "sexually transmitted disease," and "sexually transmitted infection."; VD.

Steely Dan: 1. a metal vibrator. 2. penis.

Stench Trench: a smelly vagina.

Stiffie: erection.

Stigmatophilia: a fetish for body piercings.

Stingy Nut: when a chick isn't worth sexing; pull down her pants, bend her over, and jerk off all over her ass.

Stinker: an Asshole.

Stink-Hole: the way a person's mouth smells after some ATM.

Stomach Pancakes: created when a man ejaculates on his, or his partner's, stomach.

Straight: heterosexual.

Stranger on the Rocks: the stranger, except a man numbs his hand in ice water.

Stranger: when a man sits on his hand until it falls asleep, then uses the hand to masturbate so it feels like a stranger is touching him.

Strangers In The Night: when you and your gay buddy each numb your hand, you should know how by now, and spank each other off; eliciting the feeling of a hand job from someone else, from someone else.

Strap-On: a detachable phallus, often used during girl-on-girl sexual encounters.

Street Taco: a cheap treat a man picks up on the street to satisfy his overwhelming hunger. Street tacos can cause regret, vomiting, bacterial infections, and even death; New York Fish Taco.

Stride of Pride: when a person is proud of who he had sex with the night before, to the extent that he parades around in the disheveled clothes he wore out the previous night; walk of shame.

Strumpet: slut.

Stud, Stud Muffin: an alpha male.

Stuff: sex.

Stuffing: a fat fetish in which a person eats, or is made to eat, to the point of physical pain; fat fetish, feederism, feeding, feedism, gaining, inflation, immobility, padding.

Submissive, sub, subbie: one who derives sexual pleasure from yielding control to a dominant partner.

Succubus: a demon woman who sucks the life-force from a man.

Suck Ass: when something is compared to the awfulness of performing analingus on a dirty asshole.

Suck Face: kiss.

Suck Off: fellatio.

Sud N' Fud: when trying to bang a girl, she gives that same old story, "I not that kind of girl.", "I don't sex on the first date.", "I'm catholic.", "Stop asshole.", etc. etc. After hearing all this, you whip out your handy bar of soap. Then lather up her armpit, or any other joint you prefer, and proceed to sex that instead.

Sugar Baby: the benefactor of a sugar daddy; gold digger, prostitute.

Sugar Daddy: a wealthy man who financially provides for a much younger, and considerably more attractive sex partner.

Sugar Lumps/Plumbs/Tits: small, but appetizing, breasts.

Sugar Momma: an older woman who financially provides for her younger sexual partners.

Surfing the Crimson Tide: 1. when a woman is menstruating; 2. having sex with a woman who is menstruating.

Surfing: having sex with an obese woman. So named because of the waves of flesh, the feeling of being unbalanced, and the fear of being crushed.

Swamp Ass: sweaty ass cheeks.

Swamp Donkey: an unattractive person.

Swan Sauce: a sweaty liquid of body fluid and dead skin that accumulates around the vagina.

Sweater Meat: breasts, particularly ones that are protruding from beneath a sweater.

Swimmer's Ear: when so much semen gets in an ear, there is a legitimate concern of developing an infection.

Swimming in the Red Sea: sex with a woman on her period; Cherry Dip.

Switch Hitter: bisexual; a male bisexual as he has a "bat" to play with.

Swoop & Scoop: when a woman runs a hand

down a man's chest, then cups his crotch, usually as a means of checking his penis size.

Sword Fighting: 1. when two boys simulate a sword fight with their urine streams; 2. when two men rub their dicks together. : cock rub, bumping dicks, frictation, frontism, frot, the Ivy League rub, knocking cocks, Oxford style, the Princeton Rub, tummy sticks

Sword: penis.

Sybarite: one devoted to the pursuit of pleasure; apolaustic, hedonist, sensualist.

Sybian: a powerful, mounted vibrator that women straddle.

Symphorphilia: a fetish for disasters or car wrecks, particularly watching or causing them.

Syntribate: rubbing thighs together to masturbate.

Syphilis: a venereal disease; French gout, ladies' fever, lifelong companion, Neapolitan bone ache, siff.

Sphinx: a bikini wax in which all pubic hair is removed; full bikini wax.

Superman: an absurd sex act that begins when a girlfriend or wife chooses sleep over sex. The man discretely ejaculates on his sleeping partner's back. When she wakes in the morning, the bed sheet will be glued to her back like Superman's cape.

T

A Ten: a perfect specimen of masculinity or femininity.

Taco: vagina; fish taco, pink taco.

Tadpole: man who dates older women; cub.

Tag: sex.

Taint: perineum. It ain't your dick and it ain't your asshole; Nacho.

Taking the H/B Train to J Town: a handjob or a blowjob.

Tallahassee Gas Mask: when one splatter

farts into a hotel provided shower cap and sneaks up behind a loved one and pulls it around their face like a gas mask.

Talent Scouts: Men who stand on the fringes of social gatherings staring at women without bothering to mingle or to conceal their intentions.

Talent: A woman's physical beauty; a coded Menglish term when men are describing the quality of attractive women at a party, bar, or strip club.

Tallywhacker: penis

Tamakeri: ball busting.

Tampon: man hole cover, mouth mattress, pleasure garden padlock, red flag.

Tank-Top Bodybuilder: a man who only works out his vanity muscles on his upper body and who has slender, feminine legs.

Tanorexia: a disease in which no matter how tan a person becomes, she thinks she must be tanner to be attractive.

Tantalolagnia: a fetish for being sexually teased.

Tap that Ass: sex.

Taphephilia: a fetish for being buried alive.

Tard: abbreviation for a mentally retarded person.

Tart: slut.

Teabag: to suck on a guys testicles; testicles are placed in a mouth or on a face for pleasure or as a prank. The victim of this prank is often the first person to fall asleep or pass out at a party filled with the type of dick bags who like to take photos of their genitals in a friend's mouth.

Team Cream: orgy.

Technophilia: a fetish for technology, which usually centers around cyborgs, robots, and sex machines. This fetish is often related to other fetishes, such as replacing an amputated limb with a machine, or having sex with a robotic sex doll.

Telephonicophilia: a fetish for phone sex or dirty talk.

Temptress: a woman who derives pleasure from getting men to engage in deviant activities, like cheating.

Ten Pin: a woman who has an hourglass figure and who would score a perfect ten if her beauty were judged in the Olympics.

Ten Pinter: someone who you would only consider having sex with after ten pints of beer.

Tennessee Abortion: giving birth directly into the mouth of a bear.

Tentacle Fetish: a fetish for tentacles, often depicted in hentai or other forms of animated erotica.

Tequila Golden Shower: when a person takes a shot of gold tequila which is promptly chased by being showered in urine.

Teratophilia: a fetish for deformed or monstrous people; dysmorphophilia.

Testadunattaphilia: sex with turtles.

Testalgia: any type of testicular pain or an inflammation of the testicles. Similar medical conditions include orchitis and didymalgia; blue balls, hot rocks, love nuts, stone ache.

Testicles: Male gonads housed in the scrotum; ballocks, balls, bangers, bird's eggs, clangers, cojones, cullions, danglers, eggs, family jewels, glands, goolies, jewels, love apples, marbles, nards, nuts, plums, pounders, rocks, seeds, stones, swingers.

Texas Chili Bowl: think Tabasco sauce, a telephone and the anus.

Textrovert: one whose social skills, and ability to flirt, are limited to texting.

T-Girl: transsexual girl; a genetic male who lives as a woman and who may have many of the physical characteristics of a woman, such as breast implants, but who still has a penis.

Thesauromania: a fetish for collecting women's clothes; involves collections of panties or undergarments.

Thick: 1. fat, but in an appealing way, at least to men who have a fetish for large women; 2. a penis with a significant girth.

Thigh Gap Porn: porn that features women who are either so skinny or muscular that a gap forms above their thighs and below their vagina.

Three-Hole Par: a sex session that utilizes a woman's mouth, vagina, and anus.

Threesome: group sex with three people; Triolism/Troilism.

Thunder Cunt: a woman who is so violent and threatening that it would not be surprising if her vagina carried an electric charge.

Tickle Torture: a form of BDSM in which a submissive partner is tickled, often while being bound.

Tickling Fetish: a fetish for being tickled or for tickling submissive partners; tickling often triggers some of the same muscles as orgasms; some tickling enthusiasts see the act as an expression of intimacy. Others simply enjoy torturing a partner or seeing their partner cry from forced laughter.

Tiger Stripes: stretch marks. These are as common a sighting at strip clubs as tramp stamps. When they appear around a woman's stomach, they are a good indicator the woman has, or had, a child.

TILF: teacher I'd like to fuck.

Timophilia: A fetish for wealth; chrysophilia.

Tinkering Under the Hood: cunnilingus, with specific attention paid to working under the clitoral hood in order to get the engine running properly.

Titanic: A large woman who goes down on a man their first time out.

Tits, Tittys: Boobs.

Tittoo: Tattoo on the breast, particularly around the nipples.

Titty Bar: a strip club.

Titty Fuck: when a dick vigorously slides up

and down between a pair of boobs; involves large boobs and lube.

TNA: tits and ass; refers to softcore media.

Toilet: altar room, bath, bathroom, chamber of commerce, facilities, gentlemen's room, ladies' room, little boy's/girl's room, loo, marble palace, men's/women's room, pot, powder room, restroom, sandbox, shit house, shitter, washroom, water closet, whiz stand.

Token Resistance: when a woman claims she cannot have sex with a man right before she has sex with said man in order to preserve the illusion that she is not promiscuous.

Tongue Punch: an invasive act performed by the tongue that is often unwanted; It can be used to describe abrasive kissing, cunnilingus, or rimming.

Tonsil Exam: fellatio.

Tool: 1. one who is too stupid to realize he is being used; 2. penis.

Toolbox: the tools a man uses to get under a woman's hood and attempt to rev her engine. Specifically, the dick and balls.

Tooth Whitening Treatment: when a man ejaculates in his partner's mouth.

Top Heavy: when a woman's bust measurements exceed her hip measurements.

Top Piece: to give head.

Top Surgery: when a transsexual changes their biological chest to match that of their mental gender without changing their genitals. This includes when a M2F transsexual gets breast implants and a F2M transsexual gets a mastectomy.

Top: the person who penetrates the bottom partner; also, the dominant partner in a fetishistic relationship.

Top's Disease: when a dominant partner believes the control and power he wields during fetish play extends to other areas of his life; often occurs when a top believes a bottom is actually inferior, as opposed to just assuming a submissive role.

Tortoise: any sexual act performed on a person whose pubic area is as smooth as a tortoise shell. As in Aesop's fable, you get there before the hare (hair) does.; When you eat out someone who doesn't have pubic hair yet; you got there before the hair (hare) did.

Tossing Salad: a common prison act where one person basically chows asshole with the help of whatever condiments are available.

(ex. jelly, syrup, olive oil, etc.)

Tossing a Salad: is to have an orgasm or to eat some ones ass; analingus; licking an asshole.

Town Bike: slut;. everyone gets to ride her.

Tramp Stamp: A tattoo on the lower back of a woman that symbolizes her willingness to act impulsively, such as getting a trendy tattoo or having a one night stand; also refers to wanting anal sex over regular sex.

Tramp: slut.

Tranny: Most often used as a category of porn that includes M2F transsexuals; generally considered a derogatory term, though some transsexuals embrace it.

Transformation Fetish, TF: a fetish for transforming or changing people into other people, objects, or creatures. This sexual fantasy is often limited to depictions in hentai and other forms of animated porn, though some body-modification enthusiasts do try to physically transform themselves into non-human creatures. Sub-genres of transformation fetish include: human-animal TF, object TF, gender TF, cock TF, and combining TF.

Transgender: an umbrella term for anyone

who embraces an alternative gender from that of their genetic sex; transgendered people can include cross dressers, transsexuals, drag queens.

Transition: the process of legally and medically transforming from one gender to another.

Transsexual: a person who feels that their mental gender and biological sex do not match, and who has taken medical and/or legal steps to transition from one gender to another.

Transvestite: a cross dresser, particularly a man who has a fetish for wearing women's clothing. These men are often heterosexual.

Treasure Trail: the line of pubic hair extending down from the belly button to the wider patch of pubic hair. If this appears on a woman, it is a sure sign that she does not trim her pubic hair; happy trail.

Trichophilia: a fetish for hair.

Trick: 1. a prostitute; 2. the sex acts a prostitute performs to get paid.

Triolism/Troilism: 1. Threesome; 2. a fetish for threesomes, or for watching your partner have sex with another person.

Tripsolagnia: arousal from having one's hair manipulated or shampooed.

Tripsolagnophilia: a fetish for getting or giving massages.

Trisexual: a person who will try anything when it comes to sex.

Trojan Horse: when a man covertly slips off his condom during intercourse in order to secretly unleash his soldiers inside his partner.

Troll: usually an ugly, short, fat person who is in no way sexually appealing.

Tropical Jungle: a wild pubic region that has gone untended for some time. A tropical jungle tends to be overgrown, to emanate a swampy funk of decay, and to be swarming with dangerous life forms.

Tropical Wind: when getting your asshole eaten out by a worthless tramp, and you break wind.

Trout Pout: lips obviously enhanced by collagen injection; ASLs, DSLs.

Truffle Butter: when you pull your dick out of the asshole and continue fucking her pussy, and the tan buttery substance around her pussy.

Tryke: a MTF transsexual who identifies as a lesbian.

Tuck Job: pushing your dick and balls back between your legs to form a mangina. Professional tuck jobs by cross-dressers and transsexuals often involve a layer of tight underpants.

Tug Job: a hand job.

Tummy Sticks: a kind of naked dry humping in which two men rub their erections on each other; cock rub, bumping dicks, frictation, frontism, frot, the Ivy League rub, knocking cocks, Oxford style, the Princeton Rub, sword fighting.

Tuna Can: a short, thick penis that resembles a can of tunafish.

Tuna Melt: cunnilingus on a woman after she has received a cream pie; you're down on a chick lapping away and discover that it just happens to be that time of the month. By no means do you stop though; when the whale spews tartar sauce with a hint of raspberry smothers your face.

Turd Burglar: 1. the person who slips into a public bathroom just as you are about to unleash a noisy dump. This person then hangs out for way too long, seemingly waiting to steal the turd you are forced to hold back until you are alone again; 2. a gay man.

Turkish Water Boarding: a threesome sex position that is a mix between water-boarding torture, Chinese water torture, and a Turkish bathhouse with a zany twist. One man lies on the bed with his head near the headboard. His face is covered with a pillow, bed sheet, or towel. The woman mounts the man in the cowgirl position. The second man stands over the first man's head with his back to the wall while receiving fellatio sex from the woman. The torture part comes when body fluids drip from the standing man onto the fabric covering the bottom man's face.

Turn Tricks: provide sexual pleasure for profit.

Turtle Head: when a turd begins to poke out of an asshole.

TV: transvestite; used in personal ads and in porn.

Twat: vagina.

Twink: a young, skinny, and usually effeminate gay man.

Twisted Sister: a woman or transsexual who lures straight men home in order to peg them in the ass with a strap-on or a hidden penis; have your dominatrix girlfriend dress up in some hot black leather gimp wear and proceed to handcuff your hands behind your back and then force you to your knees; unsuspecting, diminutive, and cradled over with your ass is in the air, she then gives you the most erotic enema of your life. Now that's some great S&M fun.

Two in the Pink and One in the Stink: inserting two fingers in a vagina and one in the asshole; the shocker.

Two Squeezes: a nonverbal signal between fetish players, often used by a gagged partner, to signal that everything is alright.

Two-Dick Mouth: a mouth large enough to comfortably accommodate two dicks simultaneously.

U

Udder Nonsense: playing with breasts.

Ugly Duckling Syndrome: an attractive person who bloomed late in life and still has the personality of an ugly person; used to describe an attractive person who is uncommonly nice or who dates people far less attractive.

Umbrella: while fisting an orifice, the fist blossoms open like an umbrella's spines.

Umlauts: breasts. German breasts.

Unbirthing: the sexual fantasy of crawling into a vagina. Particularly popular among furries and hentai enthusiasts. Sometimes associated with voraphilia, in which a person fetishizes the idea of being ingested. Pop-culture references: Nirvana's "Heart-Shaped Box": "Throw down your umbilical noose so I can climb right back."

Unbutton the Mutton: to take out one's penis.

Uncle Fucker: a gay man.

Unclog the Drain: female masturbation.

Under Boob: the underside of a perky set of boobs that is exposed despite the nipples being covered.

Underwear Fetish: a fetish for underwear. This usually involves men who like to smell, wear, or collect unwashed panties.

Unrequited Love: love that is unreciprocated. Also, the only type of love that endures.

Up Skirt: the view up a woman's skirt. Often refers to the illegal practice of obtaining such a view without the woman's consent.

Upper Decker: when you defecate in a toilet's water-tank; a kind of ticking shit-bomb planted as revenge during a party.

Urethra Play: the act of inserting objects into the urethra to inflict a mixture or pleasure and pain; Sounding.

Urethra: the tube that transports urine out of the bladder; in men, the pathway through which seminal fluid is ejaculated.

Urinate: to empty the bladder; bleed the liver, drain the lizard, drain the radiator, drain the snake, leak, make water, number one, pass water, pee, pee-pee, piddle, piss, shake the dew off the lily, see a man about a horse, spring a leak, squeeze the lemon, syphon the python, take a leak, take a piss, tinkle, water the horses, wee, wee-wee, whiz, wring out a kidney, wring your sock out.

Urine: what is emptied from the bladder.

Urolangia: a fetish for watching others drink urine.

Urophilia: a fetish for being urinated on or for urinating on another; golden shower; arousal by being urinated on.

Ursusagalmatophilia: a fetish for teddy bears. Also, a fetish for dressing up in animal costumes. A form of plushophilia, which is a fetish for stuffed animals; furries, plushies.

Urtication: a BDSM practice of using nettles to sting a partner's skin, causing them to develop hives. The practice was once used to treat paralyzed body parts.

Uteromania: unbridled sexual desire in a woman; nymphomania.

Uterus: where fetuses develop in the female of most mammalian species; in human females, the uterus is bookended by the cervix, which opens into the vagina, and by two fallopian tubes.

Uxorious: showing excessive or submissive affection or fondness toward one's wife.

V

Vacation Amnesia: 1. when you cannot recall what, or who, you did while on vacation without your significant other; 2. completely cutting off all communication with a person you shared a romantic encounter with while on vacation.

Vacuum Beds/Cubes: a sex toy used in BDSM, bondage play, and by latex fetishists;. a person is vacuum-sealed in one of these latex beds or cubes, leaving them breathing through a tube and completely unable to see, hear, or move.

Vagina: ace of spades, Adam's cave, altar of love, axe wound, baby gap, baby incubator, bacon strips, bear claw, bearded clam, beaver, blackberry, box, bush, cabbage patch, cake, canal street, candle holder, catcher's mitt, cavern, cellar door, clam burger, cleft, cock dock/holder/socket, cockpit, coochy, coonskin cap, cooter, cooze, crack, cranny, crawl space, crease, crevice, crotch, crumpet, cunt, danglers, dick storage unit, divine scar, downtown, dugout, eel skinner, fanny, female parts, fish taco, flower, fly trap, foofoo, fort bushy, front butt, fur, fur burger/box/pie, furrow, fuzz, kitty, gash, growler, gully hole, hair pie, hairy harmonica, ham wallet, harbor of hope, holiest of holies, honey hole, honeypot, hooha, hot pocket, juice box, kangaroo pouch, kitten, kitty, lady bits/parts, lotus blossom/patch, love canal/pudding/tunnel, lower lips, mailbox, manhole, mark of the beast, meat grinder, Medusa, Miss Nancy, muff, nanner, naughty/prick purse, panty hamster, pink taco, pleasure pit, pocket, poon, poonany, poontang, postage slot, powder box, pudding pot, pussy, quim, rabbit hole, sascrotch, sideways smile, sin hole, skin chimney, slash, slit, slot, slurry/spunk bucket, snapper, snatch, sperm sponge, stab wound, stench trench, taco, tamale, trim, tulip, tuna taco, tunnel of love, twat, vag, vagine, va-j-j, vertical smile, whisker biscuit, whispering eye, wizard's sleeve, the y, yoni/yawne, Yucatán Peninsula, zipper.

Vagina Dentata: Latin for toothed vagina; folktales and urban legends originally used to discourage men from forcing women to have sex or from having sex with foreign women.

Vagina Extender/Tightener: when a woman grips her partner's penis during penetration, fostering the illusion that her vagina is tighter and/or deeper, or to prevent the man from pulling out when he ejaculates.

Vagina Spaghetti: a hairy vagina coated in menstrual blood.

Vagitarian: one whose sexual urges are satisfied almost exclusively by performing cunnilingus on others.

Vajabond: a man who wanders from vagina to vagina, never settling in one for too long; Va-j-j, Vajayjay, Vajaja, Vjayjay: Vagina.

Vajazzle: a bedazzled vagina that looks as though it has erupted with a sparkling STD. It is not advisable to have sex with such a vagina as the rhinestones can cause serious injury. Like most lingerie, such ornaments make the person wearing this decor feel sexy, but they serve little practical purpose.

Van Dyke: a butch lesbian who drives a masculine vehicle or who is a professional truck driver; a lesbian or pre-op female-to-male transexual with facial hair.

Vanilla: mainstream sexual acts or couples.

Vart: a vaginal fart; queef.

Vasopressin: a hormone that, among other things, influences pair bonding and mate guarding in some mammals.

Vatican Roulette: the rhythm method of birth control.

V Card: membership into the virgin club. One voids his v card the first time he has sex.

Vegetarian Hot Lunch: a variation of the Hot Lunch in which the diner stretches a piece of saran wrap over her mouth such that chewing, for texture, is possible, but no actual contact with waste product occurs.

Venereal Disease, VD: Any sexually transmitted disease; STD, STI.

Venery: the search for or achievement of sexual ecstasy.

Venus with a Penis: a pre-op male-to-female transexual.

Ventriloquist: a woman who can queef on command.

Vertical Smile: vagina.

Viagra: the first and most famous pill approved by the FDA for treating erectile dysfunction; the little blue pill.

Vibrator: any sex toy that stimulates a clitoris by vibrating. A vibrator can be a dildo, but not all dildos vibrate; crotch rocket, love wand, magic wand, magic stick, marital aid, Mr. Fantastic, rubber fuckie, steely dan, weed wacker.

Vicarphilia: a fetish for living vicariously through others; involves listening to other people's sexcapades.

Vick's Vaporlove: using Vick's Vaporub to masturbate or as lube during sex.

The Viennese Oyster: from her back, the flexible bottom partner crosses her feet behind her head while the man penetrates her.

Vincilagnia: a fetish for being bound or tied up; involves a desire to feel at the mercy of another; merinthophilia.

Virgin: one who has yet to have sex.

Virginity: a state of being sexual inexperienced that some maniacs consider to be a virtue.

Virile: masculine; filled with male energy.

Voluptuary: one who is devoted to the pursuit of carnal pleasure; apolaustic, sybarite.

Voluptuous: an adjective that is used to describe a curvy woman with large breasts and or a large ass; a euphemism for a fatty.

Vomit Fetish: any fetish involving vomit. These include being vomited on, watching others vomit, or forcing oneself to vomit; Emetophilia.

Vore, Voraphilia: a fetish for being eaten alive, or eating another person who is still alive; a sexualized version of cannibalism.

Voyeur, Voyeurism: a fetish for spying on others, particularly their sexual activities.

V-Point Relationship: a polyamorous relationship in which two people have a sexual relationship with the same person, but not with each other.

Vulva: the vagina, clitoris, and labia.

Vulvodynia: chronic vulvar pain, particularly during sex.

W

Wail Away: vigorous masturbation.

Walk like Tarzan, Talk like Jane: a masculine homosexual man with a feminine voice.

Walk of Shame: the walk home after sleeping at a sex partner's house. These walkers are easy to spot as they are wearing the going-out clothes from the night before. This walk most often occurs on college campuses and is made all the more shameful by the fact that this person's sex partner was not considerate enough to escort her home.

Walrus: an absurd sex act in which a man ejaculates in his partner's mouth, then pinches her lips together, causing the semen to drip from the sides of the mouth like the teeth of a walrus.

Wang: penis.

Wank: masturbate.

Wanker: a jerk-off. Someone who masturbates constantly.

Wank Off: fuck off.

Wank Job: hand job.

War Wound: a sex injury.

Water Sports: any type of sex play that involves urine or enemas; a category of porn.

Wanton: to behave in a sexually arousing manner; used to describe promiscuous women.

Wedding Tackle: penis.

Weed Wacker: a vibrator used on a hairy, overgrown vagina that has been suffering from neglect.

Weed Whacking: smoking pot then masturbating afterwards.

Weenis: a tiny penis; pweenis.

Weiner: penis.

Well Endowed/Hung: possessing a large penis.

Western Grip: while masturbating, a man turns his hand around so that his thumb faces his stomach, similar to the grip rodeo riders use.

Wet: being sexually aroused; specifically refers to when a woman's vaginal fluids are flowing in advance of penetration.

Wet & Messy Fetish: a broad spectrum of fetishistic acts that involve making a sex partner wet and messy with various substances; includes bukkake, sploshing, goo fetish, slime fetish.

Wet Dream: a dream that accompanies a nocturnal ejaculation.

Whack It/Off: male masturbation.

Whale Eye: anus.

Whale Tail: the waistband of a thong or G-string that sticks out above the rim of a woman's pants or skirt. Like a tramp stamp, a whale tail, is a telltale sign of a promiscuous woman.

Whaling: hunting fatties. Common whaling

vernacular includes: spotting a "whale tail," "harpooning," "there she blows," and "spermaceti." While master whalers participate in this trade for sport, or as a form of bonding with fellow whalers, others take it on as a profession. If one harpoons a whale that is wealthy, this endeavor can also turn out to be financially beneficial; hogging, hog hunting, pig sticking, porking.

Whiff of Lavender: a relationship or marriage that disguises one or both of the partners' homosexuality; beard, closet door.

Whisker Basket/Biscuit: a hairy vagina.

Whiskey Dick: impotence resulting from drinking too much alcohol; the excuse men use when they cannot get an erection with a sex partner they met while drinking.

White Honey: semen.

Whore, Whore Bag: prostitute.

Whore Exchange: the collection of women's clothes left behind from a string of one-night-stands; these clothes are left by women rushing to leave or as an excuse for them to return later. In either case these garments are then donated to the whore exchange, which should consist of two boxes: small and medium. When a woman does not want to make the walk of shame wearing the same clothes from the previous night, she may search for a new outfit from the "whore exchange."; if the woman is bigger than a medium, a potato sack should be made available for her.

Whorelock: a warlock of whores; a wizard at seducing and unlocking the legs of promiscuous women.

Whoreship: the worship of whores. An affinity for promiscuous women.

Whoriental: a promiscuous Asian person.

Whispering Eye: vagina.

Wide Stance: a reference to a closeted gay man's conservative views on homosexuality; this move is a way of inquiring if another man is interested in anonymous sex.

Wife: a legal prostitute who contractually agrees to sell her services to a single man for an indefinite period of time; ball and chain, best friend, bride, companion, consort, esposa, homewench, mate, monogamist, old lady, other half, partner, spouse, wifey.

Wingman: a friend who helps you meet and seduce sex partners.

Wizard's Sleeve: a vagina that droops like an

oversized coat sleeve. Such a sleeve may have a few tricks hiding up it, but none that you want to see.

Womyn: woman, as spelled by militant feminists/lesbian who want to completely disassociate themselves from men.

Woody: erection.

Woody Allen: when a man with a dense patch of pubic hair balances a pair of glasses on the shaft of his penis.

Woofter: homosexual.

Work Spouse: a person who you develop a friendship with at work, and who you would likely date if you were both single. Real spouses often become jealous of all the time their significant other shares with a work spouse.

Worship: to obsessively adore or appreciate a person or a body part. In fetish pay, this often involves kissing, licking, or massaging a dominant partner; may be involved in the worship of specific body parts, such as ass worship, foot worship, or dick worship.

W/S: watersports; used in personal ads and porn.

WTF: what the fuck.

Walrus: after spunking in a girl's mouth, you pinch the center of her two lips together and hold her nose. This will force the cum to dribble out of the sides of her mouth, thus the teeth of the walrus.

Western Grip: when jerking off, turn your hand around, so that your thumb is facing towards you. It is the same grip that rodeo folks use, hence, western.

Woody Wood Pecker: when you are sucking on his balls, he taps his little friend on your forehead.

Westside Glaze: same as the eastside glaze, but the majority of your jizz lands on the left side of her face.

X

Xanthodont: someone with yellow teeth.

Xenophilia: a fetish for strangers or foreign objects.

Xeronisus: an inability to reach orgasm.

XXX, Triple X: used to designate something as pornographic and sexually explicit.

XDR: a cross-dresser.

Xenofuckic: just as xenophobic people are afraid of foreigners, xenofuckic people are afraid of having sex with foreigners or strangers.

Xeric: lacking lubrication.

Y

Yard Sale: when a streetwalking prostitute invites strangers to visit her lawn and handle her used goods; solicitation.

The Y: vagina.

Yank, Yank the Doodle/Crank/Plank/Yam: male masturbation.

Yearn: a feeling of sexual longing, usually for a specific person.

Yeastiality: a fetish for bread; involves having sex with warm dough.

Yeasty Buns: a large buttocks seemingly made

of leaven bread.

Yellow Fever: being sexually attracted to Asians.

Yellow Shower: urinating on someone for sexual pleasure; golden shower.

Yestergay: a person who claims they used to be gay; hasbian.

Yiffing: sexual acts involving stuffed animals.

Yodeling in the Canyon/Gully: cunnilingus.

Yogurt: semen.

Yoni: vagina; used in The Kama Sutra and by hippies.

Your Mom: apparently she is a very promiscuous woman.

Yucatán Peninsula: vagina, particularly one contained within a triangle tan-line, especially if said tan was obtained on vacation in Mexico.

Z

Zebra: 1. a white woman wearing visible black underwear or a bikini. Also, a black woman wearing visible white underwear or a bikini; 2. a person from Africa of mixed race; 3. a white or black person who behaves like a member of another he race; Oreo.

Zelophilia: a fetish for feeling jealous.

Zentai: a fetish in which participants wear Zentai suits—skintight suits made from thin, stretchy fabric—in order to have anonymous sex with other Zentai enthusiasts, or to participate in some anonymous dry humping.

Zepplins: fake breasts that are so large and

perky that they seem to be filled with helium and capable of transporting their owner through the air; Flesh Zepplins.

Zero: anus.

Zipper: vagina.

Zipper Sparks: dry humping.

Zipper Sex/Dinner: fellatio with the penis sticking through a man's fly.

Zipper: vagina.

Z-Job: an act performed by a gigolo. If you have to ask, you can't handle it.

Zombie Mask: when a man ejaculates in his partner's eyes, causing her to stumble around the room with her hands out, moaning, temporarily blind, and pissed off; While getting head from your favorite, unsuspecting, trash-barrel whore, tell her you want her to look right up at you with those pretty little eyes" when you blow your load. Then, just when you're ready to spew a good week's worth of goo, blast that hefty load in both eyes. This temporary state of blindness will produce the zombie effect as she stumbles around the room with arms outstretched, and moaning like the walking dead.

Zoophilia: a fetish for acting, dressing, and

being treated like an animal. May involve walking on all fours, wearing a collar, and eating out of pet bowls; sexually arouse by animals.

Zoosexual: one who has a sexual preference for animals.

Zwischenstufe: homosexuality; being aroused by members of the same sex

ABOUT THE AUTHOR

The author was born on March 28, 1960 in the city of Moose Jaw, Saskatchewan, Canada, and moved to Ontario, Canada where he has remained.

Between 1978 and 1981, Walter studied Film Production at Conestoga College of Applied Arts and Technology.

Walter has written a number of books and now has entered into publishing.

BOYS KILL, MEN DIE is his first foray into the realm of e-book publication, and with print through Amazon.

You can stay in touch with the author through the following:

https://www.facebook.com/walter.petrovic

https://twitter.com/**walterpetrovic**

https://ca.linkedin.com/in/walterpetrovic

personal email: srkntwp@gmail.com

websites:

http://walter-petrovic.webs.com/

http://walterpetrovic.wix.com/author

OTHER BOOKS BY THE AUTHOR

On Smashwords.com e-Books

Boys Kill, Men Die
What A Man Wants In A Woman
What A Woman Wants In A Man
Yum-Gasm: Collection of Favorite Recipes

On CreateSpace and Amazon

Boys Kill, Men Die
Freedom: Reflections On A Farce
Scorched Earth: Reworked Edition
Progressions: The Early Years (Poetry); Reworked Edition
Professor Atoz's Nasty Dictionary

COMING SOON:

Life In A Thrashing Machine; reworked edition
So, Take A Fence!
Blind In One Eye

Thanks and Reminder

Hello students of the gross and disgusting.

I am hoping that you all enjoyed this dictionary, had a few laughs, and were able to say the customary "Ewwwws!" while reading the definitions.

I just wished to Thank you all and just a request reminder—please keep an eye and ear open for other slangs, and even actual learned words and their meaning and contribute to the 2nd Edition, which will be launched in January 2017. I will give all contributors mention in the next edition.

There are a few blank pages to add your gems. Hope to collaborate.

Walter D. Petrovic
December 2016

WALTER D. PETROVIC